The Past We See Today

'In a little land like England almost every place
is marked by man, stamped with the evidence of
life, and therefore suggesting something to the
imagination.'

John Masefield: *So Long to Learn*

VICTOR E. NEUBURG

The Past We See Today

Illustrated with photographs, maps and diagrams

London
OXFORD UNIVERSITY PRESS
1972

Oxford University Press, Ely House, London W.1

GLASGOW NEW YORK TORONTO MELBOURNE WELLINGTON CAPE TOWN IBADAN
NAIROBI DAR ES SALAAM LUSAKA ADDIS ABABA DELHI BOMBAY CALCUTTA MADRAS
KARACHI LAHORE DACCA KUALA LUMPUR SINGAPORE HONG KONG TOKYO

© Victor E. Neuburg 1972   First published 1972
ISBN 0 19 273120 3

Frontispiece. 3 Terrett's Place, Upper Street, Islington. An early nineteenth-century house mentioned in Dickens' *Martin Chuzzlewit.*

PRINTED IN GREAT BRITAIN BY
MORRISON AND GIBB LTD., LONDON AND EDINBURGH

Acknowledgements

I should like to express my gratitude to Mrs. B. M. Gilbert for her invaluable help in the preparation of this book and in proof-reading.

V.E.N.

For permission to reproduce copyright material, the author and publishers wish to thank the following:

Heinemann Educational Books Ltd. for the passage from Lord Ernle's *English Farming Past and Present*, reprinted 1967; The Historical Association for the extract from M. Rix, *Industrial Archaeology*, 1967; Norman Jewson for the extract from his book *By Chance Did I Rove*, Earle & Ludlow, 1952; The Society of Authors as the Literary Representative of the Estate of John Masefield for the lines from his autobiography *So Long to Learn*, William Heinemann Ltd., 1952.

Aerofilms Ltd.: *p. 15*, Silbury Hill, Wiltshire (previously published in the B.B.C. Publications pamphlet *Silbury Hill*, 1968); *p. 29*, Wanstead House today (previously published in *The Face of Essex*, County Council of Essex Record Office, 1967); *p. 47*, Fig. g, 'ribbon development' (previously published in Michael Storm, *Urban Growth in Britain*, Clarendon Press, Oxford, 1965).
Barnaby's Picture Library, London: *p. 5*, Model of a charity-school boy, St. Bride's Church, Fleet Street, London; *p. 42*, Street scene, Swiss Cottage, London.
George Bell & Sons Ltd.: *p. 101*, Plan of the Battle of Naseby, from Peter Young and John Adair, *Hastings to Culloden*, 1964.
L. T. Blackmore, photographer, Minehead: *p. 70*, Culbone Church, Somerset.
Chartered Insurance Institute, London: *p. 61*, Leeds fire mark (one of the fire marks from their extensive collection).
Civic Trust Library, London: *p. 83*, Birmingham canal-side before and after restoration. (Photographs by Birmingham Works Dept.) Civic Trust Awards Scheme, 1969.
Clarendon Press, Oxford: *pp. 26, 27*, Plans of Leeds, from Michael Storm, *Urban Growth in Britain*, 1965; *p. 43*, diagram showing town growth, from same source.
Stuart Clark, A.I.I.P.: *p. 28*, Photograph of Leeds from Knostrop, 1964 (previously published in Michael Storm, *Urban Growth in Britain*, Clarendon Press, Oxford, 1965).
Geoffrey Cromack (freelance photographer): *p. 46*, Figs. a, c, 'Georgian terrace house', 'Victorian mock-Gothic' (previously published in Michael Storm, *Urban Growth in Britain*, Clarendon Press, Oxford, 1965).
J. M. Dent & Sons Ltd.: *pp. 97–98*, Two plans of Hastings, from C. N. Barclay, *Battle 1066*, 1966.
Euan Duff (freelance photographer): *pp. 46–47*, Figs. e, f, h, i, 'Semi-detached houses—1930's', 'Terrace houses—1930's', 'Detached houses—1950's', 'Block of flats—1960's' (previously published in Michael Storm, *Urban Growth in Britain*, Clarendon Press, Oxford, 1965).
E.R.D. Publications Ltd., Exmouth: *p. 66*, Diagram showing growth of the parish church; *p. 68*, Drawings of buttresses and columns; *p. 69*, Drawings of windows and doors, from Eric Delderfield, *Ancient Churches for Beginners*, n.d.
Essex Record Office (County Council of Essex): *p. 29*, Print of Rocque's 1735 plan of Wanstead House grounds (previously published in *The Face of Essex*, 1967).
Fox Photos Ltd.: *p. 49*, New Stock Exchange, City of London; *p. 85*, Flyover, Western Avenue extension, London.

ACKNOWLEDGEMENTS

Greater London Council Photograph Library: Frontispiece illustration of Terrett's Place, Upper Street, Islington; *p. 81*, Crystal Palace, 1895–6.

The Guardian: (First published in *The Guardian* on the dates shown.); *p. 3*, The former rum warehouse, Deptford (9.12.69); *p. 32*, Change in the Village (30.7.69); *p. 48*, Shepherd's Bush (25.2.69); *p. 86*, 14th-century inn (31.12.71); *p. 109*, Dobson's Mill, Lincs. (20.12.71).

C. J. Long, F.L.A., Borough Librarian, Hackney Library Services, Central Library, Hackney: *p. 51*, Illustrations of Homerton Row, first published in the library's *Profile*, February 1970.

Her Majesty's Stationery Office: *p. 17*, Hadrian's Wall, Housesteads. Crown Copyright. Reproduced by permission of the Controller of H.M. Stationery Office.

Pat Hunt (freelance photographer): Cover illustration of lamplighter at work in The Temple, Fleet Street, London.

A. F. Kersting, A.I.I.P., F.R.P.S. (freelance photographer): *p. 34*, 14th-century tithe barn, Bradford-on-Avon; *p. 65*, St. Andrew's Church, Greensted-juxta-Ongar, Essex.

Lincoln City Libraries Museum and Art Gallery Photographic Dept.: *p. 53*, Newport Arch, Lincoln (S. J. Harrop, Corporation Photographer).

Kenneth Lindley: *p. 74*, Village chapel, Faulkland, Somerset; *p. 75*, Methodist chapel, Snaith, Yorks., from *Chapels and Meeting Houses*, John Baker, 1969.

Roger Mayne (freelance photographer): *p. 46*, Figs. b, d, 'Victorian semi-detached houses', 'Edwardian semi-detached houses' (previously published in Michael Storm, *Urban Growth in Britain*, Clarendon Press, Oxford, 1965).

Rev. A. H. B. McClatchey: *p. 20*, Escomb Church, Bishop Auckland, Co. Durham. (Photograph by Nicholas Dowrick.)

John Mowlem & Co. Ltd.: *p. 60*, Illustrations of London Bridge.

National Trust for Scotland: *p. 102*, Culloden battlefield today, from *Culloden: A Guide to the Battlefield*, 1965.

Northern Dales Building Trust, 5 Bankfield, Kendal, Westmorland: *p. 38*, Map of Reeth, from T. B. Bagenal, *A Guided Walk Round the Buildings of Reeth*, 1968.

Norwich City Council: *p. 50*, London Street, Norwich.

Miss Sarah Orwin: *p. 24*, 'Map of Laxton Towne 1963, Mark Pierce's Map' (re-drawn by Helen Orwin from a map in the Bodleian Library, Oxford). (Previously published in Professor Chambers' *Laxton*, H.M.S.O., 1964.)

Penguin Books Ltd.: *p. 36*, Plan of Heighington, Co. Durham; *p. 37*, Plan of Coxwold, Yorks., from pp. 18 and 9 of Thomas Sharp, *Anatomy of the English Village*, 1946. © Thomas Sharp, 1946.

The Post Office: *p. 90*, Victorian letter box.

J. K. St. Joseph: *p. 12*, Maiden Castle, Dorset; *p. 19*, Silchester, Hampshire. (Copyright Reserved.)

Science Museum, London: *p. 82*, 'Wylam Dilly' locomotive.

Shrewsbury Public Library: *p. 79*, Bridge at Ironbridge, Salop, looking upstream.

Thomson Newspapers Ltd. (Photographs first published on the dates shown.): *p. 3*, Albury Street, Deptford (*The Sunday Times*, 11.2.68); *p. 44*, Police Notice (*The Sunday Times Magazine*, 16.8.70); *p. 52*, Blandford Forum, Dorset (*The Sunday Times*, 19.7.70).

Transworld Features Syndicate Inc.: *p. 34*, Tyneham Village, Dorset (previously published in *The Observer*, 25.5.69).

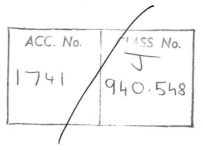

Preface

What I have tried to do in this book is to show that the search for the past we see today is an interesting and worth-while activity. It is not just a matter of reading, but involves going out and about, looking, asking and comparing as well. Some of the things to look for and to ask about are mentioned in these pages, and some of the suggestions you might like to compare with what you know already. You should look at buildings, of course, for these are amongst the more substantial memorials of the past; but do not neglect less spectacular items like post boxes and chimney-pots, for no picture of the past which you make for yourself is complete without such seemingly insignificant details.

I am grateful to my daughter Caroline for outspoken criticism and for typing the final version of the manuscript, and to Barbara Gilbert for preparing an earlier draft and for constant discussion. My wife Anne, Lydia Hoffmann and William John Fishman all read the manuscript and made helpful comments. For any errors and omissions I alone am responsible.

Contents

1   The World of William Tomkins

Some time during 1791 a silversmith's apprentice named William Tomkins complained that his master beat him unduly, and made him work on Sundays until eleven at night. The master claimed that the boy was insolent and had been flogged for this reason. These facts we learn from the *Complaint Book* of the Chamberlain's Office, which is now in the possession of the Guildhall in the City of London; and so far as written records are concerned this is probably all we can know for certain about William Tomkins.

Unlike kings and queens, nobles and statesmen, admirals and generals, ordinary folk like this apprentice left few records behind them. If, therefore, we are to understand something of the daily life led by William Tomkins and people like him—perhaps even to discover what sort of people they were—we must find other ways of reconstructing in both a factual and an imaginative way the world in which they lived. But why should it be worth looking beyond an entry in the *Complaint Book*? Is there really any reason for being interested in the lives of ordinary people in the past?

The simple answer to these questions is that any attempt to understand how people lived in bygone times is fascinating for its own sake. Apart from this, it can bring us to a fuller understanding of the world we live in today. Nothing man-made that we see around us has come about without some kind of reason. Modern houses, for instance, may be simply the result of natural development in planning, where design is constantly changing and new materials are put to use as time goes by. On the other hand, we may be able to understand after a little thought how there has been a desperate reaction against the discomforts, the lack of natural light, heating facilities and space, and all too often the squalor of many of the older buildings—and to achieve these changes in our surroundings we may think that much picturesque charm has been swept away. A decision as to whether this has always been worth it can only be a personal one.

What sort of landscape did William Tomkins see in eighteenth-century London? What kind of houses would he have known? How did he dress? These are the questions we might wish to ask, and local history can help us to answer them in a way which is not based primarily upon books, maps and manuscripts (though these are, of course, important sources), but is based upon our everyday concerns. Local history begins with our immediate surroundings. It is by looking closely at these that we can begin to study and enjoy the subject. The raw materials of local history are all around us if we have the eyes to see them.

A period building, a railway station, a remote farm, an old bridge, a cobbled village pavement, can all provoke our curiosity. Even in areas which are now heavily built up there is much to be learned from the position of the local church and the pattern of the roads. The church may have been the centre of an earlier settlement which had grown out of a village whose origins went back to the Middle Ages. What of the main roads? Certainly new roads are built, especially where there are new housing estates; but the high street and other important roads in an area may follow an age-old route. Then, too, a complex of modern buildings may be on the site of a village which was populated and thriving within living memory. Possibly farmland or even forest has been built over, and the only hint we have of earlier times, unless we go to old maps, is in the name of a street or an estate.

It is here that we shall certainly find clues; they will not always be obvious, nor always very easy to understand, but undoubtedly they can help us to see something of the past, providing that they can be puzzled out. There are books which can help us to do this, some of which are mentioned later, but a simple example will show exactly what I mean about the help that place-names can give us. At Deptford in South London there used to be an important Naval base, and the victualling yards where supplies were stored and loaded onto ships covered quite a large area. The Navy has long since left Deptford, and the yards have given place to a large

The ground floor of a former rum warehouse at Deptford, South London, now used by yachtsmen. The rest of the building has been converted into flats.

housing estate—some indeed of the old buildings have been incorporated into it and the rum warehouse, for instance, has been put to a novel use (see above). This estate is named after a man who had a great deal to do with His Majesty's ships about three hundred years ago, Samuel Pepys, better known perhaps for his diary. The estate not only commemorates his work for the Navy, but enables us to *see* exactly where it took place.

Despite rapid change and rebuilding, it is still comparatively easy in London to form a fairly accurate picture of the world of William Tomkins the apprentice. There are eighteenth-century houses to be found, and we may be certain that he would have seen dwellings like them. Not far from the Samuel Pepys estate is

3

Albury Street, where there are some houses (see below) which were probably built between 1714 and 1720. They have wood-carved door canopies which are decorated with scrolls, cherubs and ships' instruments, and while they are still to be seen—some have already been demolished—they contribute towards our picture. Then,

Eighteenth-century houses in Albury Street, Deptford, South London. Note the elaborately carved doorways.

although little in the way of physical remains can convey any sense of the bustle of London's streets in the eighteenth century, it is possible to discover what the people who thronged them looked like; and in particular William Tomkins himself would probably have resembled the model of a charity-school boy which can be seen in the Church of St. Bride, Fleet Street (see facing illustration).

There are other ways in which our knowledge of William

4

Tomkins' world can be extended. In spite of the bombing during the Second World War, a number of churches in the City of London are essentially those that he would have known, and these are worth discovering and exploring. Amongst them are St. Botolph Aldersgate, which was rebuilt in 1790 and altered again later; St. Mary Woolnoth, designed by Nicholas Hawksmoor who had been 'scholar and domestic clerk' to Sir Christopher Wren; and St. Lawrence Jewry, rebuilt by Wren in 1671–77, which was bombed in 1940 but has been beautifully restored. Then, too, 1791 was the year of John Wesley's death. His life had been a long and influential one, and he had changed English religious life in important ways, so that the passing of such a notable figure could hardly have been unnoticed by Londoners. The house in City Road where he died still stands, and is now used as a Wesleyan Museum. The burial-ground opposite, known as Bunhill Fields, has remained unchanged over centuries, and here John Bunyan and Daniel Defoe lie buried. Farther down the City Road is Finsbury Square, originally built during Wesley's lifetime as a new and fashionable estate.

Model of a charity-school boy, St. Bride's Church, Fleet Street, London.

5

An important thing to remember about William Tomkins' London is that although crowded and bustling, it was very much smaller than it is now. Throughout the eighteenth century London had been growing, but it was not until after 1791 that the great dock area was built, and railways did not reach London until the eighteen-thirties. These two developments caused a great increase in population, which itself was followed by other changes; and one effect has been that some of the country villages of those days, such as Hampstead and Highgate, have now become part of the expanding metropolis.

Taking London as an example, I have suggested some of the lines of evidence we can seek in an attempt to re-create the scene during one period of its past. Remembering that local history, like most kinds of history, is essentially about people, the solid evidence of roads, churches, houses and the like, will help to inform our imaginations about the kind of lives these people lived; and thus we can see William Tomkins not merely as an entry in the Chamberlain's *Complaint Book*, but as a boy who lived his life in a London which, despite the many changes that have taken place, can be discernible to us now.

Whatever the landscape, the task of the enthusiast for local history remains the same: to look at his surroundings, learn to recognize the sort of evidence they offer, explore it and relate it to other facts and discoveries.

By doing this, you will soon be able to draw conclusions about the past from what you see around you; but this should not lead you to disregard other sources which may support your field-work, and indeed suggest fresh lines of approach. The first of these is the public library, where it is usually possible to find a local-history collection whose librarian—often specially trained—will be glad to help you. The scope of local collections varies enormously, and may include items that you scarcely think of in connection with history, such as theatre programmes and trade directories, both of which may be useful. Can you think why?

Here are some of the things you will find in a well-organized collection. First, there will be any histories of the town or neighbourhood which have been published. A great number of local histories appeared during the nineteenth century and early in the twentieth, some of them extremely lengthy books, and not all of them of equal value; but they do provide a wealth of fact, and most of them are illustrated. The majority of their authors have been more concerned with details of estates and their owners, heraldry and genealogy than with the everyday lives of the more humble members of the community, or even with the physical growth of the town or village. However, many of these older books do have an interest, and may provide information which you cannot easily —if at all—find elsewhere.

There should also be files of local newspapers, cuttings, prints and illustrations of all kinds. The value of such material is very great, and may provide confirmation of discoveries that have been made, or suggest further questions and inquiries. In most local collections, too, there may be unprinted records which can provide valuable insights into the life of a community one, two or three hundred years ago—or even earlier. These may include record books of parish committees, known as vestries, who had charge of the running of day-to-day affairs before there were local councils. Rate books have often been preserved and so have the notebooks of those who were responsible for looking after the roads in a parish.

The word 'parish' crops up often in local history, and it is worth-while to consider briefly just what the word meant in the past. It was not only a district which had its own church, but a division of a county for purposes of administration. For this reason its records are of exceptional value. For instance, christenings, marriages and deaths have been recorded in parish registers since the time of Henry VIII, over four hundred years ago; and while not all of these early registers have survived, it does become possible, from a study of those which have, to gain a reasonably accurate idea of many of the details of family life in days gone by.

Unprinted books and documents belonging to the parish—they are usually known as manuscript sources or archives—are sometimes to be found in the local library, or in a special department devoted to their care and preservation known as a Record Office, and occasionally they are still looked after by the local vicar. It will be difficult for you to obtain access to many of them because of their extreme age, fragility and value, and quite often scholars will work from photographic copies so that the originals may be subject to less handling.

The printed and manuscript sources I have mentioned are all of great use to the local historian, but the printed material upon which the field-worker will rely most of all is the map. There are all sorts of maps, and every local collection will contain a number of them, drawn at varying times, and to different scales; what I want to do here is simply to draw attention to their general usefulness in exploring the landscape. In particular, maps of the eighteenth and nineteenth centuries may reveal some very striking facts about the ways in which town and country have developed. At the outset of any exploration you should inquire about the range of maps in the local-history collection, and it is not too expensive to buy an Ordnance Survey map of the district you wish to explore. The $2\frac{1}{2}$"-to-the-mile map will probably be the best one for you to start with, though later you may need the 6"-to-the-mile map.

Photocopying is a useful method by which maps and fragile documents can be made available for detailed study, but in order to obtain a photocopy you have to know precisely what it is you want copied. It is here that a local-history librarian can be helpful in indicating just what is available. There may be catalogues and guides; and especially useful will be any booklets issued by libraries, Record Offices or local authorities.

Museums may offer a good deal of background knowledge which can give purpose to your looking at the landscape. A number of them will be mentioned in a subsequent chapter, but whatever they exhibit, it is worth reminding ourselves that looking round museums is not an easy matter. It is tiring to look at things for any length of time, and if you are tired you easily grow bored and so lessen enjoyment of what you see. For this reason it is better to make two or more visits to a museum rather than to try to see everything at once: in this way seeing the past in a museum can be a rewarding experience.

If we have travelled some way from the world of William

Tomkins, it is because I have attempted to outline both the scope of local history and some of its sources. It is before anything else a study of the English landscape, and while written and printed sources will often support our explorations they can never provide a substitute for them. In the pages which follow we shall see how men have laid out towns, how villages were built, and how the country in which we live has been transformed in differing ways by successive generations of men who have lived and worked here.

2 How the Landscape was Made (1)

The title of this chapter may seem a little misleading. I am not concerned, except very briefly, with the geological processes and changes of climate which made these islands, but rather with the ways in which man, from earliest times, has both adapted and altered the landscape for his own purposes. It is not easy to imagine what the countryside looked like at any given period, nor is it simple to see what sort of changes there have been. The important thing to remember is that we no longer have to fight a continuing battle against our surroundings in order to live, whereas until the last century this was the natural condition of most inhabitants of these islands, as it is still in many of the underdeveloped countries today. Changes in the landscape have nearly always been made so that man would be able to *control* his environment, and they have taken place for reasons connected with either agriculture or industry. In attempting to find the evidence for such developments, we must remember that most of the past we see today will be closely connected with this progressive process of controlling the landscape, and this is true no less of earliest man than of the immediate past.

The effect of man upon his surroundings is determined by two things, the nature of the land and the climate; these are closely connected, for the crops that can be grown and the nature of animal life depend upon both soil and weather. The earliest human beings in Britain were food gatherers and hunters, wandering about the country and leaving little imprint upon it. The huts or shelters, probably made of branches or sticks, together with the game traps they used, had no permanence and were swallowed up by the forest as they moved on.

Because farming even of the simplest kind needs space, it was these farms, three thousand years B.C., which left the oldest known impress upon the landscape. Trees and bushes had to be cut down in order to provide room for the cultivation of crops—stone axes and fire were the means used to clear ground—and in addition the cattle and sheep belonging to these early farmers roamed about, and in their quest for food helped in the clearing of ground by eating plants and young shoots of bushes and of trees. Nevertheless, because of the primitive tools they used, the earliest farmers were able to tackle only the lightest kinds of soil, and the mark they made upon the landscape was a slight one.

As man became a more settled farmer, the population of these islands grew and farming became very much more varied. Pottery became familiar, bowls and drinking vessels were in daily use and so were many flint tools. For protection, camps were built on hill-tops, and these took the form of a flat open space surrounded by concentric rings of ditches and banks with wooden palisades. A number of these camps (or forts as they are sometimes called) have survived, though the timber has long since disappeared. It is still often possible to enter the camp area by the original causeway that was cut through a section of the earthworks.

Such camps and forts remain an impressive reminder of early men and their life in these islands. Many—but not all—are to be found on the chalk downs of Southern England. By far the most striking of these, though not the largest, is Maiden Castle which lies two miles south-west of Dorchester in Dorset (see illustration on page 12). Occupying a saddle-backed hill-top a thousand yards long, and surrounded by a threefold defensive system of banks and ditches, it dominates the landscape. It is now an empty shell of the settlement which once thrived on the site. Detailed excavations were carried out in 1934–1937 by Sir Mortimer Wheeler (see page 104), and have provided the evidence from which the story of Maiden Castle may be reconstructed. There was a Late Stone Age village 2000–1500 B.C., and after a gap of more than a thousand years, another settlement from roughly 250 B.C. to A.D. 70. Early Iron Age and Early Roman periods provided another occupation in the area, during which it took its present shape. In the fourth century it was partially reoccupied but by the fifth nobody seems

An aerial view of the site of Maiden Castle, Dorset.
(Photograph by J. K. St. Joseph.)

to have been settled there.

About fifteen hundred years, then, separate us from the last inhabitants of Maiden Castle, and a visit to the site is a memorable experience. The wind and the sun and the rain have done little to change the shape of the landscape, and although detailed remains of man's occupation have disappeared, many of the relics which were discovered during excavation can be seen in Dorset County Museum in Dorchester. One exhibit, which calls vividly to mind the battle fought against the inhabitants by the Roman Second Augustan Legion under the command of Vespasian, is the skeleton of a man with an arrow-head in one of his vertebrae.

The struggle between Ancient Britons and Romans at Maiden Castle was followed some twenty or thirty years later by the establishment on the River Frome of the town of Dorchester, and the two settlements, one high on a hill, and the other at a river crossing, illustrate clearly two very different ways of life. Early men, with rudimentary tools, tended to settle on high ground where the soil was light; and besides this their fortified villages and camps on hill-tops afforded them a considerable measure of protection against marauders. The Romans, on the other hand, with more advanced tools and the ability to build roads and buildings of stone, destroyed hill-forts and made their settlements at river crossings and at important junctions of the roads they built. This fact is strikingly illustrated by Maiden Castle, high upon a hill and deserted for more than fifteen centuries, while Dorchester, founded in the valley by the Romans, remains a thriving and prosperous town.

In addition to hill-forts, early man has left us the long barrows and more numerous round barrows where the dead were buried. There are more than three hundred of these around Stonehenge in Wiltshire; and indeed, this area is one of great importance if we want to see clearly the kind of landscape in which early man lived and the mark he made upon it. Not only is Stonehenge itself an outstanding monument, but not too far away is Avebury with a modern village enclosed by enormous earthworks; and close by there is Silbury Hill—one of the greatest mysteries of early life in England (see illustration on page 15). This man-made hill, rather like a grassy plum pudding turned out of its cloth, stands at the side of the Bath Road in Wiltshire. It is so large that it could fill three-quarters of Trafalgar Square, and so high that its top would reach three-quarters of the way up Nelson's Column. It is also very old—the Romans built their road *round* it! Nobody quite knows why it was built. Modern archaeologists have spent some time excavating it, but no satisfactory reason for its existence seems to have been discovered. Despite the fact that it is so large it might easily be mistaken for a natural feature of the landscape if it were not of such an obviously artificial shape.

Nearly three hundred years ago the Wiltshire antiquary, John

Aubrey, one of the earliest Englishmen to take an interest in the evidence of the past in the landscape, wrote about Silbury in these words:

'No history gives us any account of this Hill. The tradition only is, that King Sil (or Zel as the country folk pronounce) was buried here on horseback and that the hill was raised while a posset of milk was seething.'

Some of the earliest sketches of Silbury Hill were made by an eighteenth-century writer, William Stukeley, and they show us that it has changed very little since the time he wrote. He does provide us with more information than John Aubrey did, telling us, for example, that local people held a meeting on the top of the hill every Palm Sunday—

'when they make merry with cakes, figs, sugar and water fetched from the swallow-head or spring of the Kennet.'

Professor R. J. C. Atkinson of the Department of Archaeology, Cardiff University, has written about the results of the 1968–70 excavations at Silbury in the journal *Antiquity*—Nos. XLII (1968), p. 299; XLIII (1969), p. 216; XLIV (1970), pp. 313–14. According to Professor Atkinson, the building of the mound took place in four stages, apparently as a continuous process. Although the main constituent of the mound is chalk, at its base there is a layer of gravel, capped by a heap of turf and soil. This turf has yielded vegetation and insect life in an unprecedented state of preservation. From radio-carbon tests carried out on hazel twigs and other material found in the core of the mound, it has been established that Silbury Hill was built during the Early Bronze Age. Among interesting finds during the excavations was a piece of Windmill bluestone (volcanic ash). As Professor Atkinson states: '. . . the inference to be drawn is that at least some of the bluestones were already in Wiltshire some centuries before their first use at Stonehenge itself.'

If Silbury Hill, like Maiden Castle, is among the most impressive and enduring monuments of the landscape which some of the earliest inhabitants of these islands created, there are smaller sites and relics that are just as exciting. At Chysauster in Cornwall, for instance, there are the remains of an Iron Age Settlement which consisted of eight houses, and the granite rubble masonry can still be seen. Hamlets like this were all over West Cornwall, and were occupied until Roman times. Also in the far West of Cornwall, in

Silbury Hill, Wiltshire. A relic of prehistoric Britain.

the Penwith Peninsula, the remains of the fields of Celtic farms are still to be seen.

The evidences of early men which have survived are fortunately quite numerous, and many of them are now looked after by the Ministry of Public Building and Works. The fact that so many must have disappeared is often the inevitable result of the demands of our civilization for more and more land. In 1969, for example, when the runway at Heathrow Airport, London, was being extended, some remains of an Iron Age settlement were discovered. A 'rescue-dig' took place during several week-ends in the spring and early summer in order to see what could be found, and some small but interesting relics were saved before the runway covered up this evidence—perhaps for all time.

There are, then, still ways in which you may see this ancient landscape. It is a fascinating and often a very moving one— Stonehenge and Avebury are monuments which are full of atmosphere and call to mind unmistakably the lost world of prehistoric man.

It was this world that the Romans discovered when Julius Caesar landed here to make Britain a province of the Roman Empire. The Roman occupation lasted from A.D. 43 to, traditionally, 410, and in this period of roughly 367 years they changed the landscape in two important ways—and these are ways which are evident to us today. In the first place, they imposed upon a land that was both peopled and settled, a system of roads which lasted for centuries; and in the second, some of the sites of our greatest cities are Roman in origin. In England many of these place-names end in -caster, -cester, or -chester; and in Wales and North Western England names which begin with Caer or Car were founded in Roman times.

Roads and the sites of towns, then, show clearly the Roman influence. In many cases modern roads follow routes different from those built by the Romans, but a glance at the Ordnance Survey map of Roman Britain will show the network of roads with which the Romans covered Britain. Where the route followed by one of their roads is still in use it has, of course, been metalled and is quite indistinguishable from a modern construction. A stretch of the Fosse Way, which ran from Lincoln to the coast of Devon, is still used by modern traffic, whereas in Somerset this Roman road is now little more than a country lane.

Memories of Roman days in Britain are evoked by Hadrian's Wall, a fortification which ran across the North of England from Wallsend in the East to Bowness in the West. Since 1924 it has been under the care of the Government. A good deal of the Wall has survived and many excavations have taken place along its length. Besides the Wall itself, there are various fortifications and

A section of Hadrian's Wall at Housesteads, Northumberland.
(Photograph Crown Copyright.)

camps used by the Roman army, the best preserved of these being
found at Housesteads (see above illustration). A recent traveller
has described his journey to it:

'. . . you must return to Low Brunton and turn Westward along B6318
for about nine miles. All the way you are on or near the Wall, and there
is no more inspiring drive in all England. From time to time the grey
bulk of the ancient rampart rises from the dun-coloured fields like a
submarine surfacing. Then for a time it keeps company with the modern
road until you see the triple line of ditches and vallum away to the
left . . .'

Leonard Cottrell, *Seeing Roman Britain*,
Evans Brothers, Ltd., 1963; paperback
edition published by Pan Books Ltd., 1967.

A vallum is the wall of earth thrown up when a ditch is excavated. It is hard not to sympathize with the legionaries of the army who had to march, fully laden with all their kit, across this landscape, and then build their own camps and forts. Many of the Roman soldiers came from different parts of Europe, from Asia and even from the Northern shores of Africa. What can they have thought of the formidable landscape at the farthest end of the Empire? We have no way of knowing, but what we can do is to see clearly the world they created in this sometimes bleak countryside.

At the other end of these islands, there are the remains of the forts they built to guard what they called the 'Saxon Shore'. This was the coastline stretching from Brancaster in Norfolk to Portchester in Hampshire. The most important of these is at Richborough—or *Rutupiae* as the Romans called it. It was almost certainly here that the four invading legions under Aulus Plautius assembled after landing in Britain in A.D. 43. Defensive ditches built by the Romans to cover a wide area and the walls, part of which are still standing, are a melancholy reminder of the Roman past.

The ruins of Richborough Castle stand upon a small hill. In Roman times this hillock was an island in the channel of the River Wantsum, but the sea has long since receded, leaving the remains of the wall surrounded by fields, though still set against a Kentish sky.

Exciting discoveries continue to be made about the areas touched on by the Romans. In 1971 during redevelopment at Bow in East London, a Roman road and traces of a Roman settlement came to light. A few years earlier, during excavations for a car-park near London Bridge, Roman remains were revealed. As in the case of the Heathrow discoveries mentioned earlier, present-day needs demanded that these developments of valuable land proceeded. Not all discoveries, however, are in need of such hurried 'rescue'. The chance finding of pieces of pottery in Highgate Wood, North London, led to the revelation of an important site where pots were made about eighteen hundred years ago. Since Highgate Wood is protected from development, archaeologists have been able to continue their investigations over several years, digging for a month

An aerial photograph showing traces of the Roman town of Silchester, Hampshire, remains of which lie beneath the soil. (Photograph by J. K. St. Joseph.)

in the summer and then filling in their excavations.

Here and on page 53 I have touched all too briefly upon a tiny few of the evidences of Roman times which are still to be seen, and there are doubtless many which remain to be discovered. If you look at the list of books on pages 133–34, you will find several titles which will help you to make further explorations of your own.

When the Romans left these islands some time in the fifth century they had, in their occupation of four hundred years or so, left a deep imprint upon the countryside. Their departure, of course, did not mean an immediate transformation in the lives of ordinary men and women. As always, changes in the way of life were gradual, and long-established beliefs and practices were not abandoned as soon as the last Governor and his legions left. The idea of a sharp break between Roman and non-Roman times is entirely wrong. As we have seen, the tangible imprint of the Roman occupation

The little Saxon church at Escomb, Co. Durham.
(Photograph by Nicholas Dowrick.)

20

can be expressed in two words, roads and towns; and while a number of these decayed and fell into disuse after the Romans departed, in many cases the roads they laid down and the sites they chose for settlement have survived them. Thus many of our oldest cities and towns are Roman in origin: London, Chester, York, Colchester, Caerleon, Lincoln and many others are still thriving urban settlements the oldest parts of which are built upon Roman foundations. On the other hand, Silchester in Hampshire provides an example of a Roman town which has all but disappeared. An aerial photograph (see page 19) shows up the pattern of this town, which was carefully planned and occupied for at least four hundred years. Remains of it lie beneath the soil, and the little museum near by is well worth a visit.

From Roman times up until the Norman invasion is sometimes, erroneously, called 'The Dark Ages'. During this period of something more than six hundred years—twenty generations—England became largely a land of villages. Recent excavations have revealed the existence of several towns associated with Anglo-Saxon occupation, and one of these was at Thetford in Norfolk. This was an important settlement well to the north-west of the present town in its earliest phase; there was a later development south-west of the modern town which seems to have been an industrial area, and some of the material found there indicates clearly that this town had contact with foreign countries; then, as Norwich grew more important, the Anglo-Saxon town at Thetford declined. Similar traces of towns from this period have been found at Ipswich and at Stamford, and through these excavations we obtain glimpses of the Anglo-Saxon landscape.

At Escomb in County Durham, in a decaying pit village, there is a tiny Saxon church almost untouched from the time when it was built to the present day, except for the addition of windows. As the surrounding village is being rebuilt an attempt is being made to preserve something of the atmosphere which this little church, now an impressive monument to the earliest days of Christianity in Britain, can create for us.

3   How the Landscape was Made (2)

The Anglo-Saxon settlement with its villages and churches set a pattern for future developments of the landscape; but the coming of the Norman invaders in 1066 altered the details in one important respect. The churches of the Anglo-Saxons, built mostly of wood, gave place gradually to those which were built of stone. The art of building in stone developed in Normandy, and it was introduced into these islands by Norman craftsmen. In fact, the builders came both before and after the invasion. During the reign of Edward the Confessor the Abbey of Westminster was built (on the site of an earlier church) roughly a mile from the outskirts of London. Standing upon an island in what were then marshes by the River Thames, it must have seemed to men and women of the time, whose homes were dark, chilly and uncomfortable, the last word in building magnificence.

This, of course, was before the Norman Conquest. After it, Norman churches became landmarks in the countryside and so too did the abbeys which were founded in many parts of England. The exploration of churches is one of the more obvious activities of the local historian, and in a later chapter we shall see just what these buildings can tell us. The evidence about the past that they offer us will not be concerned solely with the pattern and design of the church, but may also be concerned with its position and relationship with town or village.

The pattern of villages and churches that is still to be seen is very much a part of England's history. Despite the disappearance of villages where towns have spread out and absorbed them, or where the older parts have been submerged beneath development schemes, much of the past is still to be seen, and in parts of England the fabric has remained very largely untouched through the years. Perhaps one of the finest examples of what we might call the traditional English landscape is to be found where the West of

Dorset merges gradually into Somerset. Signposts point the way to Little Cheney, Netherbury, Long Bredy and other places, all of which call rural England to mind.

There is a danger in visiting such countryside that we may be tempted to view the past in an over-romantic way, and to see the life of bygone days in too rosy a light. This can be extremely dangerous for the historian. While there is much in the past to praise—solid buildings, well-designed furniture, and the idea of craftsmanship in the manufacture of even the humblest objects like baking pots and candle snuffers—it must also be remembered that life for most ordinary folk was hard; there was poverty and sickness, to say nothing of the chill, dark winters, and generally severe conditions of life which we in the twentieth century, who are used to a standard of comfort unknown to people in the past, would find very hard to bear.

Apart from the pattern of villages, churches and farms, one other very important change took place. In Saxon times and in the Middle Ages there were no small fields as we understand them, surrounded by hedges and walls. The method of farming was very different. Each village had its own common fields, separated from each other by unploughed strips of turf called 'balks'. In each of these fields most of the inhabitants had narrow strips of land where they could grow wheat or oats for bread, or barley for beer making, or they could find pasture for their cattle. As many as thirty of them might share a field of about two hundred acres, and their holdings of long, narrow strips of land could be widely separated. This type of farming—the 'open-field system' as we call it today—is very ancient. The process by which the system was changed, and indeed the process which created much of the countryside that we see today, was called 'enclosure'.

At its simplest, this meant enclosing the open fields, or common lands, so that a small number of landowners could farm them in larger units. The 'enclosing' was achieved by means of hedges and ditches, so that the countryside took on something of the appearance that it now has.

Of course, this was a gradual process which had begun in the fourteenth century and became widespread in the fifteenth and

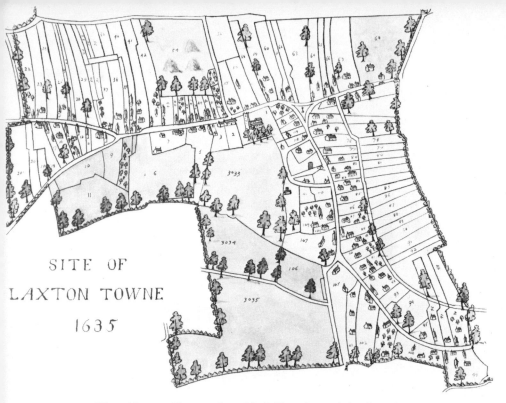

SITE OF
LAXTON TOWNE
1635

'Site of Laxton Towne 1635: Mark Pierce's map' (re-drawn).

sixteenth, leading to serious unrest in 1536, 1569 and 1607. It was, however, between 1760 and 1820 that a new wave of enclosures caused the common lands to disappear at an even faster rate, and during that period an increasing number of small independent farmers were reduced to the status of agricultural labourers.

It is still possible to see for ourselves how the open-field system worked out in practice, and what the countryside looked like before enclosure. There are survivals of it at Braunton in Devon, at Eakring in Nottingham and on the Isle of Axholme; and at Laxton in Nottingham there remains the only example of an open-field village. This means that here the life of the village is intimately bound up with the cultivation of the surrounding land, and it is not simply left to individual farmers, working quite independently of each other, to work their land as they wish.

24

The history of Laxton probably goes back to the sixth or seventh century. Enclosure certainly threatened it in the nineteenth century, and plans for this were in fact completed in 1860; but somehow it escaped. It has been suggested that the owner of the land, Lord Manvers, was too busy with the building of his huge mansion at Thoresby. As a result we have a unique historical museum, which has now been taken over by the Ministry of Agriculture with the idea of keeping it in its present state to illustrate an ancient method of farming. It is in fact a living museum, where the early history of farming may be seen at first hand. (For further information on Laxton, see J. D. Chambers' guide referred to on page 104.)

The country landscape that we see today, then, with its fields bordered by hedges and ditches, and in the North by dry stone walls, was largely created by the enclosure of common lands. We must, however, think what was the result of these changes in the landscape when they took place. In economic terms the consequence was that farming became more productive and increasingly scientific, and a larger and more varied supply of foodstuffs was grown. However, the effects of enclosure were not solely economic:

'Enclosure destroyed the inherited traditions of the peasantry, their ideals, their customs, their habits, their ancestral solutions to the problems of life—all in fact, that made up the native home-bred civilization of rural England.'

> Lord Ernle, *English Farming Past and Present*, Heinemann Educational Books Ltd., reprinted 1967.

This quotation indicates the profound change brought about in the lives of those who were dispossessed of their lands. No longer able to farm their own plots of land, from which a meagre living could be gained, they now had to work as labourers for others. Some did this, while others found their way into towns where, towards the end of the eighteenth century and at the beginning of the nineteenth, work was to be had in the ever-increasing numbers of factories which were spreading throughout the North of England and the Midlands.

The term 'Industrial Revolution' is given to the growth of the factory system and to the great changes in technology which went

Central Leeds based on a plan made in 1725.

with it. Historians are not agreed about when this process started, but there is no disagreement about the changes on the map which it produced. There were the vast concentrations of buildings on what had previously been countryside, and side by side with this tremendous expansion in building went a dramatic shift in the areas of population as men and women left the countryside to seek work elsewhere. This 'drift to the towns' has been going on for at least two hundred years and has profoundly altered the size and development of the urban centres.

Up until about two hundred years ago the chief towns of Great Britain owed their importance not to their size, but to the fact that they were important economic centres for large areas. Cities like

26

Chester had a continuity of settlement right from Roman times, while the street market at Stockton-on-Tees dates from the Middle Ages. Provincial towns provided markets where not only could all kinds of wares be bought and sold, but where servants were hired, and a great deal of business was transacted. Furthermore, these towns were important junctions on the roads which crossed the country; and at their inns the traveller could obtain not only food and accommodation, but also fodder and stabling for his horse, and even on occasion a change of horses. We shall look in a later chapter at the growth of towns in a little more detail. What I am concerned with here is the increase in town living which followed the Industrial Revolution.

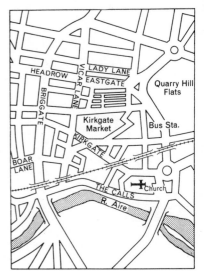

Central Leeds today.

Let us take Leeds as an example of the extent to which towns have changed. Modern Leeds, with its large population, is the product of the Industrial Revolution. The coming of factories to this city created the present-day urban sprawl. If you look at the map of its centre in 1725 (facing), you will see a great deal of countryside, planted with trees. The area now is heavily built up; certainly some of the older streets have survived, but the difference is striking. If you compare the two photographs of Leeds (page 28), one dated 1745 and the other 1964, the change is equally surprising. The church is a prominent landmark in both, but hardly anything else is common to both views.

Such developments were usually a gradual process but sometimes they came about almost dramatically, and they can present the local historian with many problems. What we have seen in Leeds is, I think, typical of all the great cities. Other changes can better be understood by looking at aerial photographs. At Wanstead in Essex, for example, housing developments border upon what was once a landscape garden. The plan drawn in 1735 (page 29) shows its intricate pattern, and the aerial photograph

Above: View of Leeds from Cross Green, Knostrop. (From an engraving made in 1745.)

Below: Photograph of Leeds from Knostrop, 1964. (The viewpoint is lower than that of the 1745 engraving.)

next to it shows us some glimpses of the original layout long after the estate has disappeared.

The housing shown in the Leeds photograph is typical of the development which took place as the great towns spread, but there are other ways in which the Industrial Revolution changed

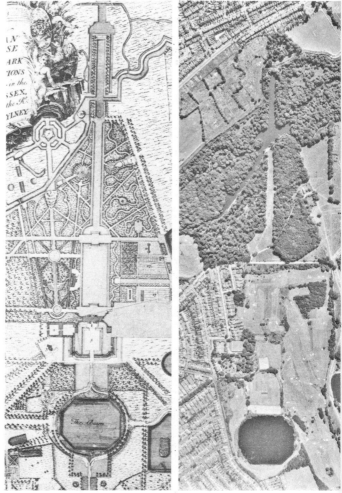

Left: The grounds of Wanstead House, Essex, in 1735.

Right: This photograph shows that even today traces of the original layout can still be seen from the air.

29

the face of the countryside. Both canals and railways cut deeply into the land. At Stoke Bruerne, in Northampton, there is the Waterways Museum which displays over two hundred years of canal history. As part of a national transport system, canals are out of date, although on the bigger waterways with port connections cargo is still carried on the barges, or 'narrow boats' as they are called. At the museum there are many relics of the waterways system, and the brightly coloured full-scale reconstruction of a barge cabin helps us to picture the lives of men and women of long ago who lived and worked on the canals. Prints, photographs, maps and documents, traditional possessions which belonged to boat-folk—a finely coloured Measham teapot, handed down from mother to daughter, is an example—suits, dresses, bonnets and skirts, together with specimens of decorative lace and crochet work from boats' cabins, bring the canal age vividly to life. There is also a fine selection of notices. One of them, more than a hundred and twenty years old, threatens with transportation any vandals tampering with the works on the River Sturt Navigation. Then, too, there are the notices which wrongdoers themselves were required to have printed, in which they apologized publicly for their wrongdoing and promised not to offend again.

Another transport system which is now undergoing considerable change is the railway. The nineteenth century was the golden age of its development and the spread of railway lines linking towns, cities and ports. Today, as we shall see later, the railways are very much less important than they were; stations are being closed and track is being taken up. Happily, however, much still remains to remind us of the nineteenth-century railway age.

A fascinating reminder of it is St. Pancras Station in London, the only major station in the capital which has remained unaltered since it was built. The Midland Railway Company decided upon this site in 1845, and during subsequent building operations the young Thomas Hardy, who later became famous as a novelist and then as a poet, was assistant clerk of the works. The builders had to dig through a graveyard, and Hardy was asked years later by his boss, Blomfield: 'Do you remember how we found the man with two heads at St. Pancras?'

The most striking thing about St. Pancras Station is the great Gothic-style hotel building which overlooks the Euston Road. There are great pinnacles, arches, a clock tower and an approach for vehicles which sweeps up from the roadway. Inside there are more than five hundred rooms, which are now used as offices; but despite this, the building is a marvellous example, both inside and out, of Victorian building on the grand scale—one of the few which are left to us. It is a genuine survivor from the nineteenth century, and it is interesting to compare its decoration and archways with the modern concrete buildings which are springing up all along the Euston Road.

All the main-line London termini are worth looking at. Liverpool Street, for example, has some beautiful ironwork in its roof, almost as though the architect were attempting to imitate the style of a cathedral in metal instead of stone. Platforms one to ten are the oldest parts of the station, and you will notice that these platforms and tracks are below the level of the street. Victoria Station, too, is of special interest: you can easily see that it is in reality two stations in one. Two companies, the London Brighton and South Coast Railway and the London Chatham and Dover Railway, pooled their resources to build this dual terminus which was opened in 1860.

Railway stations contain a large number of features which date back to the Victorian age in which they were built. London's stations have been well written about in John Camp's book *Discovering London Railway Stations*, Shire Publications, 1969. Outside the capital, you may well find it hard to establish many facts about your local railway station, whether it is a halt or a large terminus. If you are seriously interested it is worth while to send your query, enclosing a stamped addressed envelope, to British Railways Board Historical Records, 66 Porchester Road, London, W.2. If there is a branch of a local railway history society near your home you could well address your query to them in the first place, for local knowledge and enthusiasm can so often provide the information that you want.

Change in the Village.

4 The Village

In many places looking at the history of villages has been made
very difficult, partly because so many of the older buildings have
been replaced by new ones, and partly because new housing
developments at the outskirts have bitten deeply into surrounding
farmland besides changing the original shape of the village beyond
recognition. Despite this last fact, it is a good idea to look at the
history of a village by trying to discover what its original boun-
daries were, and what was the relation of the village site to main
roads and the railway. If you look at the drawing 'Change in the
Village' (above), you will see the kind of thing which is happening
to so many villages today.

32

However a village has changed and probably still is changing, it is important to know something of its origins. Consider first of all its name, its site and its form. Every settlement must have a physical origin. Early men, as we have seen, tended to settle on higher ground and it was not until there were improved methods of farming that cultivation took place in valleys and in other lowland areas. The origins of many villages are lost in antiquity— prehistoric men, Romans, Anglo-Saxons, they all have left their mark upon sites. Evidence of this may be found in place-names, and you would be well advised to look at *The Concise Dictionary of English Place-Names* by Eilert Ekwall, which will be available at your local library. This is a fascinating book, an absolute mine of information, and the search for the past of a village can be begun by consulting it.

The physical shape of the village may be harder to trace because so much of its past has disappeared, but there are still unspoiled villages in these islands. In any case the first question to be asked is this: What has determined the site and the form of the village? Proximity to a water supply—river or spring—is of immense importance. Perhaps a site was chosen because it was at a convenient cross-roads, where tolls might be levied upon travellers; perhaps a market set up to serve the immediate neighbourhood developed into a more permanent settlement. Alternatively a collection of rude huts might well have become a prosperous village simply because a castle or abbey was built near by, or there was a thriving local industry.

The variety of reasons for the founding of a village is reflected in the immense differences in the villages themselves. So many of them are beautiful, and their appearance is the result of continuous historical change over the centuries. A number of Dorset villages have preserved their rural charm and have remained fairly unspoiled: Cerne Abbas is a fine example. On the other hand, the village of Elstow in Bedfordshire, where John Bunyan was born in 1628, has now become little more than a suburb of the town of Bedford. In Gloucestershire there is Chalford, a lovely stone village near Stroud. In East Anglia, many of the villages with their fine churches are reminders of a time when the Eastern

33

counties were some of the wealthiest in England because of the prosperous cloth trade.

One characteristic of nearly all early villages was that of *compactness*, for all the inhabitants had to be within walking distance of their daily work in the fields or tending cattle. From this necessity

Nobody lives at Tyneham Village in Dorset. It has been preserved because it is in an Army training area.

there arose two basic village forms, the square and the street. The first was so called because it consisted of buildings grouped around a green, a pond or a market-place. If you look at the map of Heighington in County Durham on page 36, you will see a very good example of a plan of this kind of village. You may often find other forms, rectangular, triangular, or oblong, in which buildings are grouped round a central feature, but the term 'square' village is accurate enough to describe them.

The street village, on the other hand, is very much more rudimentary—and, of course, in days gone by very much more difficult to defend against a marauding enemy. The village of Coxwold in Yorkshire, of which there is a map on page 37, shows very clearly what this kind of village looks like. Basically the houses are strung out along the sides of a road, but a feeling for the lie of the land and

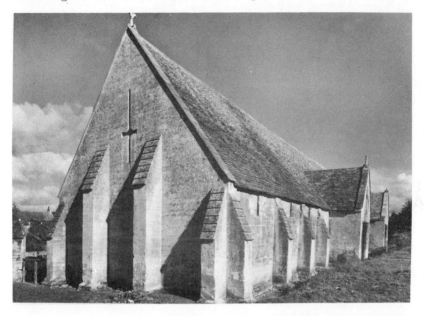

A fourteenth-century barn at Bradford-on-Avon, Wiltshire. It was used for storing and threshing grain. The buttresses keep the walls from pushing outwards under the great weight of the roof. Holes in the walls and gables let in light and air. (Photograph by A. K. Kersting.)

the planting of trees can prevent too much monotony, and, of course, there will in most cases be houses in side roads which add variety to the pattern.

One of the important things to remember about looking at the buildings in a village is that, until fairly recently, local materials were used in the construction of houses, cottages and other buildings. There were sound reasons for this. The carriage of stone, bricks and timber was very expensive, and in any case roads were unsuitable and canals few; but more important, each district in

35

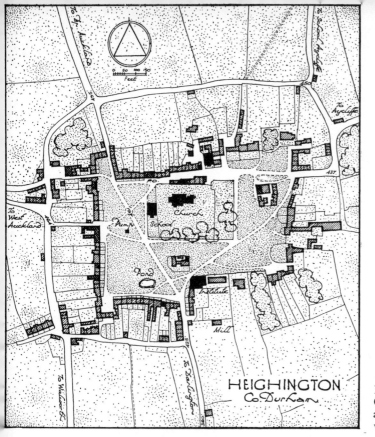

HEIGHINGTON
Co. Durham

Plan of Heighington, Co. Durham, an example of a 'square' village.

England had its own building materials and its own local skills. It is this which accounts for the quite extraordinary variety of domestic architecture to be found in the English countryside.

The change in traditional ways of building has been going on for a long time. It became most obvious after the First World War. As Norman Jewson said of building in the Gloucestershire:

'After the 1914–18 war it was soon found that these simple ways had gone for ever. Many of the older and most highly skilled craftsmen had died or retired, while the younger men returned from the war had no sympathy with the old ways. Much of the traditional skill in building was gone, while with the coming of the motor lorry brickwork became cheaper than stone, and all kinds of manufactured materials were much more easily obtained. So it became more and more difficult and expen-

36

sive to build in the old way, new cottages were built of brick and roofed with concrete tiles, barns were re-roofed with corrugated iron and there were many other innovations, until it soon became rare to find a village still entirely built of local materials.'

By Chance Did I Rove, Earle & Ludlow, Cirencester, 1952.

With this in mind, let us look at the buildings of a specific village, Reeth in Yorkshire. It takes its name from an Old English word meaning 'stream'. If you look at the plan on page 38, you will see at once that it is a square village, with the buildings set round a central green. In order to take in the general character of the village it is best to start on the Green, in front of the Burgoyne Hotel. This is an eighteenth-century building, built originally as a private house. Its imposing central door and the symmetrical rows of five windows on the second and third floors are typical of the age when it was built, and it possesses the qualities of grandeur and regularity.

Because there are eighteenth-, nineteenth- and twentieth-century buildings in this village, it is possible to make all kinds of interesting comparisons. Langhorne

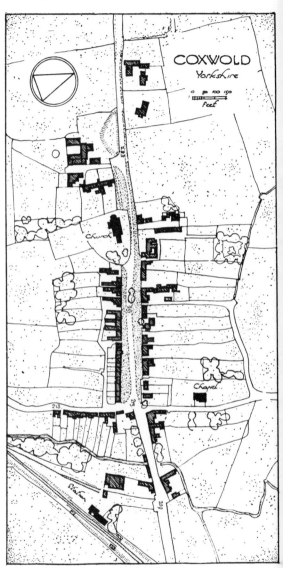

Plan of Coxwold, Yorkshire, an example of a 'street' village.

37

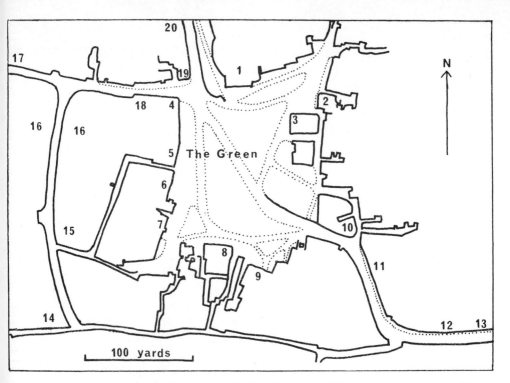

1 Burgoyne Hotel; 2 Methodist Church; 3 Vicarage; 4 Langhorne House;
5 King's Arms Hotel; 6 Black Bull Hotel; 7 Barclays Bank; 8 Literary Institute;
9 Congregational Church; 10 The Laurels; 11 Newsagent; 12 Police Station;
13 To Reeth Bridge; 14 Langhorne Lodge; 15 Old People's Bungalows;
16 Council Houses; 17 To the School; 18 Fire Station; 19 Buck Hotel;
20 Arkengarthdale Road.

Map of Reeth village, Yorkshire.

Lodge, for example, (No. 14 on the plan) is a more modern house
than those round the Green, but since it was built using stones from
a derelict building, it has a 'weathered' look.

Some of the modern bungalows have larger windows than is
usual in the older houses. This is because there is no longer any
need to keep windows small in order to prevent loss of heat, neither
is it necessary today to build so that the walls take the weight of the
roof, thus making large windows impossible. New techniques in
building have radically changed the appearance of houses.

Roofs, too, can be interesting. Artificial slates provide an often striking contrast with the more traditional stone slab slates. The Methodist and Congregational churches in Reeth exemplify this. The former, built in the Dales tradition in 1882, retains a far greater sense of dignity than the latter which was built in 1868 using Welsh slates for the roof.

Windows, doors, roofs, walls—all can tell us a great deal about buildings. Apart from noticing local building materials it is not wise to generalize too much about looking at buildings. If you are interested in the history of a village, the best method is to prepare a plan of it. Number each of the more important buildings and indicate clearly at the side of your plan what each building is, and then your investigations can begin. A visit to the local library to check on the origins of the village name and its early history is necessary at the outset. When you have established some facts, then you can look seriously at individual buildings. So far as church and chapel are concerned your quest will be an easy one, but when it comes to private houses this will prove more difficult.

These are the questions to which you will seek an answer:

i) When was the house built?
ii) Has it been altered in any way?

Of course, there is no easy method of finding an answer to either of these questions, but the following general considerations can be useful. In England, the South East and the Midlands tended, until the eighteenth century, to be more advanced economically than the rest of the country. Three factors caused this: the siting of the all important cloth industry in the South, the nearness of the Continent with its markets and commercial contacts, and the influence of London. From about 1750 to 1914 the pace of industrial expansion tended to reverse this process, so that a terrace of houses built in a Lancashire manufacturing town in, say, 1860 may be very similar to such a terrace built in Reading perhaps fifty years later.

One of the most important things to remember is that most medieval houses have disappeared and not many houses you will come across are earlier than about 1570. Between about 1570 and 1640 the wealth of the Tudor age showed itself in the tremendous amount of development which went on in the Midlands and the South East—or the Lowland Zone as it is called. After about 1660 rebuilding spread to the North, to Wales and to the West Country. The major rebuilding and development of Northern England, South Wales and London, however, dates from the Industrial Revolution which began in the late eighteenth century. A very large number of the houses—perhaps most of them—in these areas were built between 1810 and 1910.

With these general ideas in your mind, it becomes easier to answer the questions already asked. For older houses, it is best to consult M. W. Barley's *The English Farmhouse and Cottage*, Routledge, 1961. Taking the period from about 1575 to about 1720 the author covers the country region by region. You should find a copy of the book in your local library. For later houses you will have to look elsewhere, and again the library may be of great help. A book you should certainly look at there is John Woodforde's *The Truth about Cottages*, Routledge, 1969. This short, very well illustrated volume should enable you to identify at least roughly the date of village dwellings you may come across.

Used in conjunction with reference books your own observations can be invaluable, but great care is needed for many old houses have been altered, and have had features added to them so that they are in fact the product of several periods in history. Large windows, for example, may be added to a cottage which originally had small ones, and often in the process of rebuilding, little except the foundations may be left of the original fabric of the house.

One of the most valuable aids to your own observation can be a tithe map. These were produced when church tithes in kind (chickens, hay, pigs, eggs) were changed into money payments after 1836. The scale of these maps was usually twenty-five miles to one inch and the tithe map is often the earliest map of the settlement. If there is such a map for the village you are studying, the local Reference Library will know about its existence and may even have a copy of it. There should be three copies altogether, one at the Public Record Office in London, the Bishop's copy—usually now at the County Record Office—and the third with the parish. This is the one that you may find in your library.

There is no doubt at all that the exploration of a village will provide you with a challenge, and a great deal of ingenuity and hard work may be required before you are able to see its past. Do not be afraid to look for books and maps to confirm what you see, and to provide you with ideas and information.

There are three other publications which you will certainly find of value. First, Joscelyne Finberg, *Exploring Villages*, Routledge, 1958. This is a well-illustrated and clear account of villages and what you can expect to find in them. Look through this book and read the chapters which interest you most.

The second is Dennis R. Mills, *The English Village*, Routledge, 1968. The aim of this book is to enable you to carry out your own investigations into how a village has developed. There are some extremely useful maps and a few illustrations.

The last one is a pamphlet: Nigel Harvey, *The Story of Farm Buildings*, Young Farmer's Club Booklet No. 27 (Evans Brothers), 1953. There are thirty-three illustrations in this excellent guide to a very complex subject. Since farms are first of all work places, and are privately owned, it is not always easy to obtain permission to inspect one. If you are lucky enough to do so, this booklet will be invaluable. There are some other interesting titles in this series, covering such subjects as farm tools, horses, cattle and so on.

Swiss Cottage, London. Note the conglomeration of traffic signs.

5 Looking at Towns and Cities

If you look at the diagram on the next page, you will see that over the last one hundred and seventy years or so the population of towns and cities has so increased that today less than a quarter of the population lives in the country. We are thus a nation of town dwellers, and for this reason probably take urban surroundings very much for granted. The picture of Swiss Cottage in London on a winter's day (above) shows clearly what a jumble of unrelated items such surroundings can be. If we look more closely at it, however, there are one or two clues to the study of the past even here.

First we are reminded—by no less than four signs—of the immense importance of roads. The reason for so many signs is that there is so much motor traffic which has to be directed at this point where several roads come together. Not one of these road signs has the simplicity of a roadside milestone, like the one on Highgate Hill where Dick Whittington is said to have sat as he listened to the sound of Bow Bells; but these modern signs are a development of the earlier ones, more complex because there is so much more traffic now than there was in the past.

Milestones and guide posts served road users until the Locomotive Acts of 1861 and 1878. Heavy steam engines and road rollers made their appearance on the roads some time after 1858, and because they were so heavy, owners of bridges were allowed to put up signs warning drivers that the bridge would not bear the weight of these huge machines.

Such notices were made of cast iron and some can still be seen on bridges, though many of the original ones were replaced later in the nineteenth century. The popularity of cycling caused a number of cyclists' organizations to put up signs from 1893 onwards—there were 3,200 by 1902—all over the country. The first warning notices of a steep hill were erected at Muswell Hill in London—notices now long since disappeared. Such signs are extremely rare; so too are those which followed the appearance of the motor-car at the turn of the century. The increasing speed of cars meant that warnings of danger were more necessary, and an Act of Parliament in 1903 gave local authorities permission to erect these. Thus even road signs have a history, although it is not yet a very well documented one. 'Belisha'

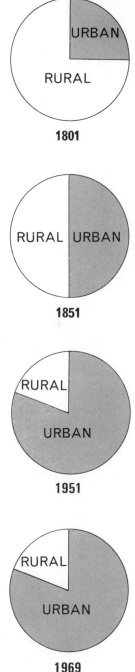

1801

1851

1951

1969

The changing urban-rural balance of the population, 1801–1969.

beacons date from 1934, and white lines on the road from 1914.
Returning to the picture of Swiss Cottage, the workmen's lamps

A police notice warning the public of traffic lights—'street crossing signals'—
outside the Houses of Parliament in 1868.

on the left are a reminder that landscapes are always changing and human settlement is never finished once and for all. The blocks of flats, bus-stops and road-traffic all indicate the complex pattern of people and institutions which go to make up a town or city.

No traffic lights are visible in the Swiss Cottage picture but there are, in fact, several sets just beyond the bus-stop. They too have a history. The earliest, which were gas-operated, were installed outside the Houses of Parliament in 1868 and a Police Notice, showing how they work and informing the public of their use, is shown opposite. Unfortunately, after a short period in use they blew up and a policeman was killed. This accident discouraged further developments and it was not until the coming of the motor-car that some kind of control became necessary. Modern traffic lights are an American invention: the first were put up in Cleveland, Ohio, in 1914. Four years later they were used in New York, and it was in 1925 that they first appeared in London. They were erected at the junction of St. James's Street and Piccadilly, controlled from a hut in the middle of the road by a policeman. The very first automatic signals were installed at Wolverhampton in 1926, and they remained in use until 1968.

Buildings can tell us a great deal about the history of a town; certainly not everything, but this is quite the best way to begin. Some of the changes in house design are illustrated on pages 46–47. The Georgian terraced house has a sense of grace and dignity that is entirely lacking in the Edwardian semi-detached house. On the other hand, where such Georgian houses have been turned into flats in overcrowded neighbourhoods, they can quickly have a seedy and run-down look. In many towns the pace of change ensures that there is no stagnation. So much of the old has gone, to be replaced by newer buildings. This process, which comes about in response to various human needs, is not always a bad one. The slum-clearance programmes in such cities as London, Liverpool, Manchester, Birmingham, have removed many buildings which were most insanitary to live in and could not even be called picturesque. The quality of change is graphically illustrated on page 48, which shows development in progress at Shepherd's Bush

45

g

h

i

Changing patterns in house design.
a. Georgian terrace house.
b. Victorian semi-detached houses.
c. Victorian mock-Gothic.
d. Edwardian semi-detached houses.
e. Semi-detached houses—1930's.
f. Terrace houses—1930's.
g. Ribbon development—1930's.
h. Detached houses—1950's.
i. Block of flats—1960's.

in London in 1969, and the size of such tower blocks is made clearer when we look at those which are beginning to dwarf the Bank and the Royal Exchange in the City of London (see page 49).

Sometimes, however, the process of change in towns is more subtle, and much of the past is preserved and can be seen if we know how to look for it. Let us look at three examples of ways in which elements at least of the past have survived.

The first is Norwich. If you look at the picture of London Street

47

on page 50, the first thing to come into mind is that here is a city street without any cars. This means that in part of the city it has become possible to see the proportions of the buildings, and to enjoy them without the noise and inconvenience of traffic in

narrow streets. Norwich is a very ancient city and in the sixteenth and seventeenth centuries it had an importance it has since lost. Because of its age, it has a large number of old buildings, and some of these can be seen in more leisurely circumstances now that traffic has been banished.

Next, Hackney in London. If you look carefully at the two pictures illustrating Homerton Row in 1886 and 1970 (page 51) you will see that the past has not entirely disappeared. The road has been widened, and the right-hand side is entirely different. On the left, a row of eighteenth-century houses has almost disappeared, but some things have remained. Can you pick out any other survivals from the past?

Old and new London: Shepherd's Bush.

48

Skyscraper blocks dwarfing the Bank and the Royal Exchange in the City of London. The new Stock Exchange building on the left of the picture is 321 feet high.

Then there is the Haymarket in London. On the west side nothing of old London is left, but on the east the Theatre Royal still looks as it did, several houses have escaped change or re-development, and Nos. 3 and 4 on the corner of Suffolk Place are almost intact. At the beginning of the nineteenth century No. 3 was an Italian warehouse, and No. 4 formed the premises of Coleman, a cutler and slate master. Today both buildings have been taken over by the American Express Co. Farther up, Nos. 33 and 34 remain as they were. So changes have been made piecemeal —and they are not always easy to discern.

There are towns like King's Lynn in Norfolk possessing a harmony which the larger cities conspicuously lack; but unfortunately such examples are becoming fewer. Some years ago it would have been possible to describe Blandford Forum in Dorset as a small town which possessed both harmony and atmosphere.

London Street, Norwich. Because cars have been banned, it is possible to enjoy the buildings and the proportions of this part of the city. Compare with the photograph of Swiss Cottage on page 42.

It had remained virtually unaltered since the eighteenth century, when it was rebuilt after a disastrous fire; but today much of its historical attraction has become difficult to discover. The gradual process by which an attractive Georgian town deteriorates is the result of careless and unimaginative local planning. In Blandford, a supermarket, a one-way traffic system with coloured road signs, an industrial estate and petrol stations have all helped to destroy the character of a lovely town. You can see how some of this has come about on page 52, and this is typical of so many of our smaller towns.

In the larger cities the survival of old buildings is more or less a matter of chance, for the pace of redevelopment and the consequent destruction of the past proceeds very quickly. Even smaller places like Dorchester have suffered to some extent from the desire to erect new buildings at the expense of old, and a failure to preserve anything of the fabric of the past. This is not in any way to claim that change in towns and cities is a bad thing, but it is a matter for considerable regret that all too often no pictorial record of old buildings is kept, and that in so many developments little attention seems to be paid to the harmony

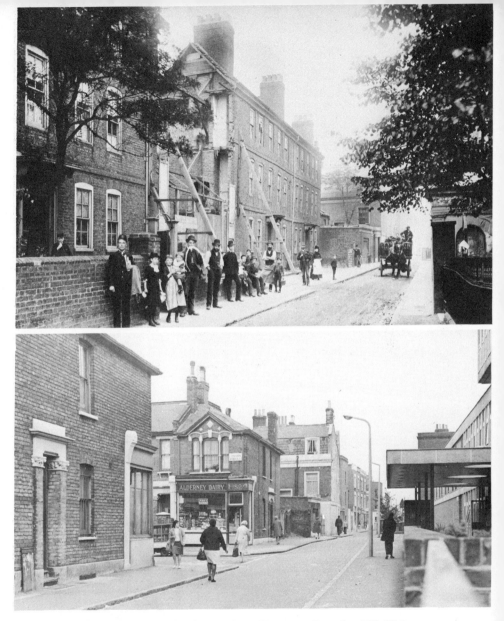

Two views of Homerton Row, Hackney. *Above:* Homerton Row in 1886. This photograph shows the demolition of the eighteenth-century houses in order to construct this end of Halidon Street. *Below:* Homerton Row today.

51

Blandford Forum, Dorset. A one-way traffic system, petrol stations, a super-market and an industrial estate have helped to spoil the charm of this Georgian town.

of new buildings with their existing surroundings. It is here that the local historian has a valuable part to play, for a record ought to be made of buildings which are to be destroyed, and this is something that can easily be done with a camera.

Let me illustrate what I mean. On the outskirts of the city of Leicester, near the football ground, there were, until a few years ago, a number of streets of late Victorian terraced houses which were demolished in order to make way for improved housing. It is excellent that people should have higher standards of comfort, but it does seem a pity that whole streets can disappear without any record, because houses like these were the homes of working men and women, and we cannot reconstruct their lives unless we have an accurate picture of their dwellings. Had the houses been of the seventeenth century, no doubt some sort of record would have been kept; but the past of the last hundred years or so is often too lightly destroyed.

As we have seen, the history of towns begins with the Romans who founded the first ones. Physical remains of their towns are rare—the Jewry Wall Museum at Leicester; 'Newport Arch', the oldest gateway still in use in Britain, at Lincoln (see below); and the Roman baths at Bath. Roman towns were carefully planned on a grid system, but hardly a trace of this remains today. As mentioned in Chapter Two, a very much surer guide to a Roman foundation is in the place-names -chester, -cester, -caster, -caister, from the Latin 'castra' meaning camp. There are several sources which can be of help with this problem: Ekwall's *The Concise Oxford*

Newport Arch, Lincoln. A relic of Roman Britain.

Dictionary of English Place-Names, which I have already mentioned, the Ordnance Survey's map of Roman Britain, and of course a visit to the town library's local-history collection will certainly throw some light upon Roman origins, if any, of a specific place.

After the Romans had left these islands at the beginning of the fifth century, their way of life largely died out and many of their towns fell into ruin. Some form of town life, of course, probably existed in London and perhaps in other larger centres; but in general the Saxons, Jutes and Angles who took the place of the Romans were farmers who had little taste for town dwelling.

It was the Norsemen who revived town life; for them the fortified town was a centre of trade and a convenient place from which to dominate the land they had, in places, overrun. In using towns for these purposes they set an example to the English, who were not slow to use Roman sites and to found their own settlements. Towns which date from about the end of the ninth century and the beginning of the tenth are as follows:

LARGE TOWNS—MEDIUM TOWNS:—
Barnstaple
Bath*
Canterbury*
Colchester*
Dover*
Hastings
Rochester*
St. Albans*
Southampton*
Southwark (now part of Greater London)
Tamworth
　* Previously Roman towns

SMALL TOWNS:—
Bredy—probably Bridport, a name meaning Bredy's port
Bridgnorth
Buckingham
Cricklade
Hertford

Maldon
Malmesbury
Shaftesbury
Totnes
Towcester
Twynham—now Christchurch
Wallingford
Wareham
Watchet
Wilton

COUNTY TOWNS:—
Bedford
Cambridge (a village in Roman times)
Chester*
Chichester*
Derby
Exeter*
Gloucester*
Hereford
Huntingdon
Lewes
Leicester*
Lincoln*
Northampton
Nottingham
Oxford
Shrewsbury
Stafford
Warwick
Winchester*
Worcester (a village in Roman times)
York*
   * Previously Roman towns

LOST TOWNS—settlements which were towns but no longer exist:—
Axbridge   (Somerset)

Burpham   (Sussex)
Chirbury   (Shropshire)
Eastling   (Kent)
Lydford   (Devonshire)
Portchester* (Hampshire)
Tisbury   (Wiltshire)
    * Previously a Roman town

This list is by no means complete. In Saxon times, for instance, Bristol was involved in the slave trade with Ireland. In East Anglia, Ipswich, St. Neots and Thetford were important centres of the pottery trade at the same period.

The most general considerations about the foundation of an old town are these. First it would be designed for defence or for trade, possibly even both. Its inhabitants would require food and water, and also a firm foundation upon which to build. Nearness to a river was a key factor for three reasons: a river provided the water supply, it provided a means of transport when there were few roads, and it could be a means of defence because it constituted a barrier to an invading army. It is no accident that 'bridge' and 'ford' occur in the names of so many early towns. The town of Stamford, for example, is situated at one of the few spots where the River Welland could be forded, while the River Thames and the River Cherwell join at Oxford.

Your best source for looking at the site of a town is the 2½″ Ordnance Survey Map (that is, two-and-a-half inches to every mile on the ground). This will show you the lie of the land, and of course whether it is flat or hilly, and it is worth recalling here that so far as defence is concerned one of the best sites for a castle was on a hill. Not only did this give the best position for a view of the country, but it could not be overlooked and would make things difficult for any attacker. Occasionally this consideration of defence outweighed all the others, and the water supply was insufficient. Shaftesbury in Dorset is a case in point. This is a very old town indeed, built upon a sandstone hill, and there was no adequate water supply there until 1868. The origins of Battle, Sussex, lay first of all in the abbey which Duke William built to celebrate the victory over the Saxons. Outside the gates a market was started, and round the market-square houses were eventually built. This was the beginning of the town and the pattern of its early development can be seen by anyone visiting the town today.

After considerations regarding the choice of site, what can we see now of a town which has some history? Naturally enough, it is not often that you can expect to see many physical remains of its origins. The local museum may have a few examples of ironwork, pottery or something similar, but you will often have to rely upon the reference library for information about the town's earliest days. Where relics of antiquity do exist—fragments of Roman or medieval wall, for example—you will find that they are cared for and preserved; and there are some exceptional instances, like Lavenham in Suffolk or Steyning in Sussex, where houses some four hundred years old can be seen. Unfortunately, although, by reason of the time-factor, buildings of the last two centuries are more likely to be still in existence, these are rather taken for granted and all too little thought seems to have been given to their preservation.

A wretched example of this neglect of the fairly recent past is to be found in London. Near Liverpool Street Station is the district of Spitalfields, which has a history stretching back more than nine hundred years. At the close of the seventeenth century large numbers of French Protestants, known as Huguenots, settled in London; many of them lived in this part of London where they became established in a number of crafts, notably weaving. This French influence is still to be seen in place-names of the neighbourhood, Nantes Passage, Duval Street, Fleur-de-Lis Street, Fournier Street. The last named street possesses a number of superb weavers' houses all with individual early Georgian doorways. You can still see the large windows let into the roofs so that weavers at their looms had the benefit of as much natural light as possible. These houses survive, but in a very sorry state; and the interiors, some with finely proportioned rooms and wide stairways, are used as factories and as offices. The lack of interest taken in these examples of early eighteenth-century town houses by the local authority is sad. In Fournier Street and in some of the neighbouring streets a fragment of an earlier London remains in disrepair and neglect.

Not so Christ Church, Spitalfields, built early in the eighteenth century by Nicholas Hawksmoor. This is being splendidly restored after suffering damage during the war, and rightly enough, but the refurbished church offers a striking comparison with the lack of interest taken in the houses of the same period.

Despite this gloomy picture, there is a great deal of pleasure to be gained from looking at the old buildings of a town or city. The only way to do this is to walk round the streets, starting preferably in the oldest part of the town. If you are able to compare a modern street map with an earlier one—inquire at your library—you will get some idea of how the town has most changed. It is worth while remembering too that while buildings may have disappeared, street patterns have often remained little altered, and sudden twists and turns in the older streets may be due to the need to avoid some obstacle or building which has long since disappeared. Old guide-books and directories, especially if they are illustrated, can help you here, and these can often still be found quite cheaply in second-hand bookshops. Don't neglect the advertisements which are nearly always found at the back, for they will call to mind vividly the way of life of generations of town dwellers in the nineteenth century. The advertisement for 'Hobden's Royal Artillery Bath Establishment' (opposite), which came from an old Sussex directory, reminds us of a time when the bathroom which most of us take for granted today was not found even in many well-to-do homes.

Houses are often difficult to date precisely, and many buildings are a mixture with various features added to an existing older structure. Islington Green, a shopping centre in North London, is an example of this. Many early nineteenth-century and Victorian houses have now become shops. This transformation has come about in most cases by simply putting a shop front into the ground floor. This means that at street level there is a twentieth-century shop, but if you look above this, you will see the second and third-floor façade of what was once a family house, usually in bad repair but easily recognizable.

A word of warning. You may come across a building with the sign 'Ancient Lights' upon it. This is not necessarily an indication of antiquity, but means that the owner has a right to natural light

An advertisement in *Melville & Company's Directory and Gazette of Sussex*, published in 1858.

which may not be obstructed. This was laid down in an Act of Parliament in 1832, which also said that if such a right had existed for twenty years then the law would assume that it had always done so, and might so continue.

Many windows were bricked-in as a result of the window-tax imposed during the reign of William and Mary. The Act was not repealed until 1851, and if you come across such filled-in windows they can be another rough guide to the dating of a building.

Twentieth-century developments — supermarkets, blocks of flats, office blocks and so on—you will make out without difficulty. The past is as simple to recognize but not to identify. Precise identification is, I think, less important than the realization that old-fashioned buildings should not be regarded simply as quaint or picturesque, but can be, and indeed often are, thoroughly serviceable today. To establish the dates of houses and streets, you will have to consult early copies of a local directory. The picture of differing houses on pages 46–47 gives a rough idea of various styles, but the richness to be found in many an English town is so immense that each one must be looked

HOBDEN'S

ROYAL ARTILLERY

Bath Establishment,

Half a mile from any of the town drains,

OPPOSITE THE BATTERY,

KING'S ROAD, BRIGHTON.

The Nobility, Gentry, &c., are respectfully informed that the above Baths are fitted up with every convenience and comfort, with separate Dressing Rooms, and a Suite of three Baths, communicating with each other, when required, on giving a short notice.

AN ABUNDANT SUPPLY OF HOT LINEN.

Experienced and obliging Attendants.

LONDON AND BRIGHTON PAPERS.

A PRIVATE WAITING ROOM FOR LADIES.

Portable Baths prepared at any part of the Town.

Shower, Hip, Sponging, and all kinds of Portable Baths, Let on Hire on Moderate Terms.

WATER SENT TO ANY PART OF THE TOWN.

All Subscriptions to be paid in advance, when Tickets are given, which are transferable.

FURNISHED APARTMENTS.

59

Above: The 1831 London Bridge shortly before it was dismantled in 1967.
Below: An artist's impression of the present London Bridge. (Photographs by courtesy of Mowlem.)

at separately. Three or four examples of this variety are as follows.

The early nineteenth-century house in Terrett's Place, Islington (see frontispiece), where Dickens' Tom Pinch is said to have stayed, is one. Situated in a tiny court with no access to traffic, the house and its surroundings look much as they must have done more

60

than a hundred years ago. The main street of Henley, Oxfordshire, is another. Its width tells us that it was once used as a market-place, and it curves gently until it reaches the parish church. The buildings are of different periods and different styles, but in spite of this, there is very little that seems out of place. At Ledbury in Herefordshire there is a lane, or 'gunnel' as it is called locally, which leads from the high street to the parish church. The cobbles and the old buildings, some with timber frames, make this a living example of the kind of street where many townsfolk lived in the past. Lastly, the old and the new: the fact that there need be little conflict between them is indicated in the example of Winchester in Hampshire, where a successful attempt has been made to create new buildings without disturbing the harmony of this old town.

One of the excellent practices set in motion by the London County Council, and continued by its successor, the Greater London Council, was the placing of commemorative tablets on buildings connected with famous people. Some of the older tablets have a chocolate coloured background, while the newer ones are usually blue with white lettering. As buildings disappear, so do the tablets. An example of this is a house, located in Percy Circus near King's Cross, which bore a tablet commemorating Lenin's residence there in 1905, and which was demolished in 1970. Constant research ensures that fresh tablets are affixed

Leeds Fire Office Insurance Mark. Made of lead, this fire mark shows a ram's fleece with three stars above, from the Leeds city arms. The fleece indicates the city's old staple trade, the stars are from the Danby arms (Lords of the Manor).

61

to sites newly discovered, and you will find it worth while to look at the pamphlet called *Commemorative Tablets*, published by the Council.

In looking at old houses, principally in London, you may see Insurance Plates (also known as Assurance Marks or Fire Marks). In the eighteenth century, when houses were insured against fire the company providing the insurance also maintained a fire-engine in order that fires could be dealt with. This protection cost much less than the company's liability if the premises were destroyed by fire. The plates, usually made of uncoloured lead, showed clearly the badge of the insuring company, almost always at first-floor level. A pair of clasped hands was the mark of the earliest company, founded in 1696; while later ones included the sun and a phoenix. The purpose of these badges was this. If a house caught fire, neighbours would know which company's fire-engine to summon; and, of course, the badges were also a guide to the firemen, besides representing an early form of advertising. The firemen themselves were recruited from Thames Watermen, who undertook this task as a kind of spare-time job; and from 1821, such firemen were given protection by Parliament from being forced by the Press-Gang into Naval service. There are some interesting relics of early fire fighting in the Chartered Insurance Institute Museum at 20 Aldermanbury in the City of London. A fire mark from their collection can be seen on page 61.

To sum up, towns are living things, and their main purpose must be to serve the needs of those who live in them, but this does not mean that the past need be wantonly destroyed. Unfortunately much of value has been torn down, and what has replaced it often seems tasteless and dull when compared with earlier buildings. Often, too, as we have seen, old houses are used as workshops or offices, or have been utilized as rented rooms and flats. The fact that nineteenth-century slums and inconvenient terraced houses are being replaced is excellent, but all too often a fine building is destroyed to make way for a supermarket, and the past is totally neglected. However, much remains to delight the eye and quicken the imagination. For a long time to come, both London and provincial towns and cities will provide ample and exciting opportunities for exploration by the local historian.

6   Church and Chapel

It is difficult today to realize just how important a part religion played in the lives of men and women in the past. The parish church was in a very real sense the centre of local religious life. More than this, it was often the centre of social life, and from the year 1538, in the reign of Henry VIII, the parish priest had been responsible for keeping a record of births, marriages and deaths. Parish officials, often meeting in the vestry of the church, carried out many of the tasks which are now the responsibility of local government. Their duties in connection with the upkeep of roads and bridges, dispensing charity, arranging apprenticeships and so on, entailed a good deal of paper work, and parish records are an important source for historians today. Most of such documents are now kept in County Record Offices. Some counties, notably Kent and Essex, have published selections from the records they hold. Kent County Council in particular, in a series of books entitled *Kentish Sources*, has published material from a wide range of documents covering most aspects of day-to-day life in the past.

Churches, then, have played an important part in the life of the country; and while the church building remains as a tangible reminder of earlier days, there is very much more to the study of churches than the buildings themselves, although it is with this aspect of the subject that I am concerned in the present chapter.

Not all churches, of course, are very old, but the number of ancient ones still to be seen is surprisingly large. In fact, of about sixteen thousand parish churches in England more than half were built since the seventeenth century, and of these most were erected in the nineteenth and twentieth centuries, although sometimes incorporating, or copying, parts of the original fabric.

How ought we to look at an old church? What especial features should we be looking for? The questions 'What?' 'How?' and 'Why?' will provoke more satisfactory responses if one or two things are borne in mind.

The first thing is that most of the older churches will be a mixture of styles, with a great deal of overlapping. The basic periods of church architecture are these:

Saxon	7th–12th centuries
Norman	1066–1190
Transitional (Norman—Early English)	About 1157
Early English	1200–1300
Decorated	1280–1350
Perpendicular	1370–1550

This is a rough classification, and should be used only with the qualification in mind that styles and methods of building often tend to overlap, so that a church commenced in, say, Norman times may well have been added to at several later periods, resulting in a mixture of building styles.

The simplest styles of churches were the Anglo-Saxon. A wonderful example of such a church that I have mentioned earlier (see page 21) is to be found at Escomb in Durham. The windows were inserted long after the church was built, and in the north wall there is an inscribed stone from the near-by Roman fort at Binchester. Over the porch there is a curious sundial. The church is illustrated on page 20. This tiny Saxon church, at the bottom of a steep hill, with a simplicity almost untouched since it was built, is a remarkable building and conveys a strong sense of the continuity of life in these islands.

There is another fine early church, St. Laurence, to be seen at Bradford-on-Avon in Wiltshire. The original church was built in the twelfth century and was enlarged and altered in the fourteenth, fifteenth and sixteenth centuries. It is beautifully set in a little town which is full of lovely buildings, rising steeply in tiers from the river. Although built in Saxon times, this church was lost sight of until 1856. It was surrounded by buildings and a house had been built into the west front. The chancel arch had been pulled down and the bricks used to make a chimney stack; in the porch there

St. Andrew's, Greensted-juxta-Ongar, Essex. The only surviving example of a Saxon church in timber. (Photograph by A. F. Kersting.)

was a staircase, and a part of the church had been used as a school since 1715. The Vicar, Canon Jones, rediscovered the church and in 1871 it was bought back from private owners and preserved as an ancient monument.

One other very early church is St. Andrew's at Greensted-juxta-Ongar in Essex (above). This is the only surviving example of a Saxon church in timber; the walls of the nave are made from split oak trees. Unfortunately the building was 'restored' during the nineteenth century, but the trees amongst which this church is set add greatly to its atmosphere.

Such really old churches are rare—each of these three is, in its way, unique. The basic plan of nearly every church, though, dates from one of the types used in the twelfth century, usually with many subsequent additions.

The development of churches is quite simple, and if you look at the diagrams below and on pages 68–69 you will see how the

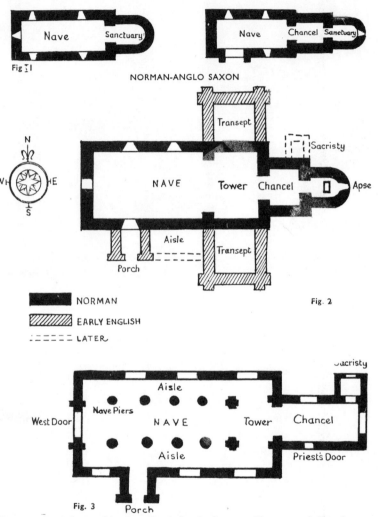

The growth of the parish church. 1) Anglo-Saxon—Norman. 2) Developments of the twelfth and thirteenth centuries. 3) A typical church developed from Norman times.

simplicity of the earliest churches became more complex as churches grew larger in response to growth in population, and as building techniques improved.

The earliest churches consisted of a covering for the altar, and shelter for the congregation. With the arrival of the Normans churches increased in size, and throughout the twelfth and thirteenth centuries further additions were made.

As rebuilding and development of churches went on, so builders became more ready to experiment, and the very thick walls and tiny windows of Saxon and Norman days gave way to thinner walls and larger windows. This in its turn created fresh problems, for if walls were thinner, what was to take the stress of the roof?

The answer was the buttress, basically a pillar built against the wall in order to support it. The earliest ones, built by the Normans, were simple in design, but they tended to become more ornamental as time went on. In the first quarter of the thirteenth century flying buttresses were used to support the upper walls of the church, and these too were simple at first and later became very ornate.

Other supports for the church building were the columns which held up the roof, and these too, as shown on page 68, began simply and grew more elaborate. The bare quality of the Anglo-Saxon column gave way to Norman, Early English and Perpendicular styles, each more ornamented than the last.

Windows are an important feature of a church. The half circle in the Norman window on page 69 is characteristic, and the English windows come to a point. As methods of making glass improved, and it became more readily available, windows increased in size. Sections of glass separated by vertical bars of stone provided the opportunity not only for larger windows but also for decorations, depending upon a pattern of glass and stone, and known as tracery, at the top of the window. See, for example, the perpendicular window on page 69. The use of painted glass dates from the fourteenth century; but Queen Elizabeth I ordered that all paintings on glass should be destroyed as 'superstitious'. Most of the coloured windows you will see are very much less old than the church. There is a fine example of early painted glass in the church of St. Mary the Virgin, at Fairford in Gloucestershire, but this is

| SIMPLE NORMAN | EARLY ENGLISH
(Flying Buttress) | DECORATED | PERPENDICULAR
(Flying Buttress) |

| ANGLO SAXON | NORMAN | EARLY ENGLISH | PERPENDICULAR |

Church buttresses and columns.

unusual, and in old churches the most satisfactory guide to the approximate date of the windows is their shape and pattern.

The same is true of doorways. Those built by the Normans have

68

the half circle, often richly ornamented at the top of the door, and later periods are easy to identify if you look at the examples below. Here again, what is necessary to remember is that much rebuilding of churches has gone on over the ages, and because a door or a window looks old it does not necessarily mean that the church is old. It may in fact date from the eighteenth or nineteenth century.

NORMAN   EARLY ENGLISH   PERPENDICULAR

EARLY ENGLISH   DECORATED   PERPENDICULAR

Church windows and doors.

Fortunately churches are amongst the best documented of buildings, and you will be wise to seek information about the foundation of the church and its subsequent rebuilding from a leaflet, booklet or notice inside the church itself. Unusual features

Culbone Church, Somerset. England's smallest parish church.
(Photograph by L. T. Blackmore.)

inside the church, too, will certainly be noted, because those who are responsible for churches are always glad to show their treasures or unusual features. England's smallest parish church, for example, is at Culbone in Somerset (see above). At All Saints, Hereford, there is a fine specimen of a Jacobean pulpit; at St. Mary Steps in

Exeter a splendidly unusual clock; and there is a Charles I coat-of-arms in the little church of Boconnoc in Cornwall. In some churches—All Saints, Northampton, and St. Bride's in Fleet Street, London, come to mind—there are representations of children in the dress of their period. In Southwark Cathedral there is a monument to Susanna Barford, who died in 1652 at the age of ten. The unknown writer of her epitaph wrote:

'This world to her was but a traged play;
She came and saw't dislik't and passed away.'

Susanna's memorial is actually within the cathedral, but churchyards too are fascinating to look at. Some of the older tombstones are beautifully carved, and there is always the chance that you may come across an epitaph illustrating one of the oddities of human life which are so often overlooked by historians, and yet which bring men and women of the past close to us. This is an example from Dorchester in Dorset:

'Frank from his Betty snatch'd by Fate,
Shows how uncertain is our state;
He smiled at morn, at noon lay dead—
Flung from a horse that kicked his head,
But tho' he's gone, from tears refrain,
At judgement he'll get up again.'

Or this one from Stepney in East London:

'Here lies the body of Daniel Saul,
Spitalfields weaver—and that's all.'

A vivid reminder, this, of the men who earned their living as weavers—a trade that has long since vanished from the East End of London.

Apart from the splendours of the parish church, be on the look-out for the curious and the unexpected. Alms-boxes, bells, bibles, brasses, carvings, chests, clocks, gargoyles, hour-glasses, musical instruments, lofts, tombs and monuments, are only a few of the things that you may come across in a church; and as I have said, the churchyard can be full of interest too. Besides epitaphs, you may happen upon sundials, crosses and vases, weathercocks, each of which may be a survival from the past.

Very similar to a churchyard is the burial-ground of Bunhill Fields, in Finsbury, close to the City of London. As mentioned on page 5, a number of famous people, including John Bunyan, author of *The Pilgrim's Progress*, and Daniel Defoe who wrote *Robinson Crusoe*, are buried here; and from the seventeenth century until 1852 the area was used as a burial-place for nonconformists— dissenters as they were called—who had no wish to be buried in parish churchyards. A visit today to Bunhill Fields is an unforgettable experience, for this patch of greenery set amongst the traffic and new buildings makes a fascinating comparison between the old London and the new. The comparison is made more interesting because John Wesley's house and a large Methodist chapel—not the original meeting-place of Wesley's followers—are near by, and so is the Headquarters of the Honourable Artillery Company which still provides volunteer soldiers in period costume, armed with pikes, on state occasions. Bunhill Fields remains much as it was in the past. Many of the carved inscriptions have weathered so badly that it has become impossible to read the original words, but this garden is well maintained by the Corporation of London and remains as a memorial to the nonconformist tradition.

Nonconformity, dissent or 'chapel' as it is perhaps more popularly known, has been a part of the religious life of this country for more than three hundred years. Many of the chapels and meeting-houses in which the various groups of Baptists, Congregationalists, Wesleyans, Quakers and others met, have survived and some are still in use.

They provide us today with a view of religion in this country's history, when the division between 'church' and 'chapel' was not just a matter of worship but of politics as well. In their origins chapels were simply meeting-places for the early nonconformists, and they have few of the artistic traditions which have gone to the making of the parish church. Differing kinds of ornamentation have given a richness to many churches—royal coats-of-arms, noble tombs, tablets displaying the ten commandments, parish chests, memorials, all have helped in this—which is entirely lacking in nonconformist chapels. Another factor, as we have already noted, was that the church was the centre of communal life over a long period of time. Chapels, on the other hand, became the centre of nonconformist life only in the eighteenth and nineteenth centuries.

Simplicity, then, is the keynote of early chapels. This does not mean that they are dull; far from it, they illustrate patterns of life since the seventeenth century in a remarkable way. The very simplicity of these early chapels demonstrates the dislike of outward show felt by many of the early nonconformists. It was not until late in the nineteenth century that chapels really became quite often ornamented, so that the development of the chapel has been from dignified simplicity to over-ornamented buildings which are unmistakable.

Unfortunately, while the parish church has been much written about, very much less has been said regarding chapels. This may prove to be a positive advantage to the local historian, however, because it is a field in which it is possible to make real and exciting discoveries. In many towns, as nonconformist sects grew in numbers during the nineteenth century, so more and more chapels were built. Many of these have now fallen into disuse, or more likely are used as factories or warehouses. Often they can be readily identified from the outside by the remnants of their ornamented façades, so that the search for 'lost' chapels can be a fascinating one.

This is particularly true of an area which developed greatly during the nineteenth century. In Islington, North London, for instance, there are several buildings now used as workshops or storage places which may well originally have been chapels, and await rediscovery. At Burnham in Lincolnshire there is a chapel, no longer used as a place of worship, which has become a hoarding for advertising posters.

The majority of chapels which can be seen today were built in the nineteenth century, although earlier ones exist. A lovely example of a seventeenth-century chapel is to be found in Tewkesbury in a tiny street opposite the Abbey, and perhaps it is this very positioning which accounts for its being often overlooked by visitors. There are some examples of period furniture and most unusually, the library of books belonging to earlier ministers has been preserved.

Basically a chapel is a rectangular building with a front which is more striking than the other three sides. The front will have an imposing door, large windows, and often some information about the chapel itself, such as name, date, and so on. Often there is a forecourt which has replaced a graveyard no longer used, and

Village chapel, Faulkland, Somerset. (Photograph by K. Lindley.)

Methodist chapel, Snaith, Yorkshire. (Photograph by K. Lindley.)

there may be a porch and a flight of steps. This kind of pattern is still recognizable under the increasing use of ornament which was used as the century progressed. Another feature which is often very striking indeed is the use of carved lettering to proclaim the name of the chapel. At Staithes in Yorkshire the word BETHEL is carved over the entrance, and at Pembroke in Wales WEST GATE CALVINISTIC METHODIST CHAPEL is carved upon a stone scroll above the door. Often dates are carved in this way, but the date you see may represent the date when the chapel was rebuilt and not that of its original foundation.

At Faulkland in Somerset there is a beautiful chapel built in

75

stone (see page 74). If you compare it with Snaith Methodist Chapel in Yorkshire (see page 75) you will have a good idea of the differences that can be found in nonconformist chapels.

Amongst some of the most impressive chapels are the one at Louth in Lincolnshire, with its high windows and the great sense of dignity which comes from the restricted use of ornament upon a fabric of brick and stone; the Old Meeting House at Bedford, with its great solidity and its connections with John Bunyan; and the chapel at Watchet in Somerset which, with its unusual curving lines and clear lettering, is a building of exceptional grace and character.

It would be very easy to prolong a list of chapels, but not useful. As I have said, considerable variations exist, and if you have a taste for old churches you should extend it to take in chapels as well, for both church and chapel have played a vital part in the lives of ordinary people in the past three centuries.

Here are some books which may help you in your quest. John Betjeman (Editor), *Collins Guide to English Parish Churches*, London, 1958, is a very comprehensive, useful book indeed. If you want something simpler which you can slip into your pocket, Eric Delderfield's *Ancient Churches for Beginners*, E.R.D. Publications, Exmouth, Devon, no date, is excellent. Finally there is Kenneth Lindley, *Chapels and Meeting Houses*, John Baker, 1969. This is an excellent guide to nonconformist chapels and has seventy-two photographs.

7 The Industrial Revolution

The Industrial Revolution is the name given to the process by which England changed from being a country where most people earned their living from the land, to one where factories and industry provided a way of life for the majority. Although historians are not altogether agreed about its origins, we can take the second half of the eighteenth century as a starting point. Of course there had been factories before this, and a shipbuilding industry; Sussex iron had been famous for centuries; houses, churches, cathedrals were built; pottery and glass were made; coal and various metals had been mined. What gave the Industrial Revolution its especial importance was the fact that industry and technology became the most important features in the life of the country.

The consequences of this were that the lives of men and women were transformed, and so too was the map. As local historians, it is this last point which concerns us most, but before we examine some of the ways in which the landscape was changed, and what we can see of this today, let us consider, briefly, what were the changes in the daily life of ordinary men and women.

By about 1800, the most obvious one was that more and more of them were becoming town dwellers, particularly in the industrial centres of the North of England—Manchester, Sheffield, Wigan, Preston, for instance. Here they earned their living as factory workers rather than as rural labourers. Whether in fact their standard of living went up or not as a result of the Industrial Revolution is still debated by historians; what is certain is that there was a great difference in the *kind* of life they led. Agricultural tasks which had varied with the seasons and the weather gave way to the repetitive, mechanical work of the factory. In due course factory conditions helped to create new demands on the part of workers for political organizations and for education, and through political and educational agencies the lives of working men were further transformed.

What, though, of changes on the map? Where are we to look for evidences of the Industrial Revolution which shattered the old agricultural world and created, gradually, the one that we know today? Before attempting to answer this question we must become familiar with a term that local historians have come to use within the last fifteen years or so—Industrial Archaeology. This is 'recording, preserving in selected cases, and interpreting the sites and structures of early industrial activity, particularly the monuments of the Industrial Revolution' (M. Rix, *Industrial Archaeology*, The Historical Association, 1967, p. 5).

Let me give three examples of relics which have survived. The first of these is at Coalbrookdale in the Severn Gorge, Shropshire. It was here in 1709 that Abraham Darby became the first man successfully to smelt iron with coke, a process which made possible the large-scale production of iron. Without this, the Industrial Revolution would have been impossible, for the earlier method of using charcoal instead of coke produced only small quantities of low-grade iron. The site was extremely suitable. High temperatures were needed for this process and the existence of a brook meant that water power was available to work the large bellows whose blast provided these temperatures; also available near by were coking coal, iron ore and the necessary labour; finally, the closeness of the River Severn—in the eighteenth century one of the busiest commercial routes in Europe—meant that finished products could be transported easily to distant markets. Some of the first productions of the Coalbrookdale Company were domestic cooking vessels, and in 1767 it produced the first iron rails. Wooden rails had been in use from the beginning of the seventeenth century, and these enabled horses to pull heavier loads than were possible on the bad roads of the period; but iron ones were a distinct improvement and were in use for more than half a century before the opening of the first railway line.

By good luck, much of the pioneering work done at Coalbrook-

78

dale survives. In 1959, to celebrate the 250th anniversary of Abraham Darby's firm, a modern company, Allied Ironfounders, gave £10,000 so that the site of the original works could be laid out as a museum. The Old Furnace is still to be seen below the dam which held back the water which worked the bellows.

The second relic is the world's first cast-iron bridge, at Iron-bridge, Shropshire, which was erected in 1779 by the Coalbrook-dale Company (see below). What is of especial interest is that various parts of the bridge are fitted together using the technique of the carpenter. Unfortunately this bridge is now in danger of collapse, but funds are being raised so save it by the Ironbridge

The first cast-iron bridge in the world. Erected at Ironbridge, Shropshire, in 1779 by the Coalbrookdale Company.

Gorge Museum Trust. To support the bridge's foundations the Royal Engineers will lay a concrete bed across the River Severn.

Finally there is the work of Charles Bage, whose flax mill, built in Shrewsbury in 1796, is now used as maltings by a local brewer. Bage was the man who replaced timber in building by metal, and his five-storey mill has brick walls with an interior framework of cast-iron pillars which support cast-iron beams on which the successive storeys are laid. It is the earliest building to have several storeys and an interior framework of iron. Originally there were five such buildings in various parts of the country, but today the one in Shrewsbury, Marshall's Mill, is the sole survivor.

These are three outstanding memorials to an industrial past, and they emphasize the importance of two things which made rapid technical change possible: coal to provide power, and iron from which machinery was made.

It is in the field of industrial archaeology that the local historian can have an especial part to play, because so many relics of industrialism have disappeared completely unrecorded. Museums cannot, of course, house everything, neither is it possible, nor even desirable, that everything should be preserved; but the destruction of the past ought not to be left to chance as it so often is. The job that the local historian can do is to see that every site or monument is at least recorded, for many of those which have so far survived will continue to be threatened.

Famous amongst those monuments which are lost is the Crystal Palace, which was burned down in 1936. Originally put up for the Great Exhibition in 1851, this was the first prefabricated building to be made from glass and metal. The fire which destroyed it was accidental, but the railway arch which was built at Euston Station in 1838 was quite deliberately destroyed in the early sixties when the station itself was being rebuilt. Fortunately an arch built at the same period at Curzon Street Station, Birmingham, still survives, but the loss of metal-framed buildings, railway locomotives and early machinery is a matter for great regret. Simply because a home could not be found for her, the 'North Star', a railway locomotive built in 1837, had to be broken up in 1905.

It would be pleasant to think that in the sixty-five years or so

Crystal Palace, London. Built for the Great Exhibition of 1851, it was destroyed by fire in 1936.

since this act of destruction better sense had been learned, but this is still not always the case. Many monuments are being threatened today with extinction or with alteration, and this is particularly true when we consider railways, canals and roads. Fortunately there are railway museums and the Waterways Museum at Stoke Bruerne in Northamptonshire; and there are also societies of railway enthusiasts, and the Inland Waterways Association, besides the Railway and Canal Historical Society; but in spite of this, more needs to be done. The railways were one of the marvels of the nineteenth century and perhaps did more than anything else to change men's way of life. They were pioneered in this country and we can be glad that some of the earliest relics are preserved here. There is 'Wylam Dilly', one of the oldest railway engines, built in 1813, which is preserved in Edinburgh (see next page); the oldest railway station, built in 1830, is Liverpool Road, Manchester;

81

while the oldest railway bridge is Causey Arch, Durham, built in
1727 long before the railway track was laid over it.

As the railway system is being radically altered today, many
buildings and sites connected with its nineteenth-century days are

One of the earliest railway engines: William Hedley's 'Wylam Dilly', built in
1813. (Photograph copyright Science Museum, London.)

left derelict, lines are closed, the stations fall into decay; and the
fast pace of change gives an urgency to the task of recording the
past as well as seeing it.

The canal system faced the same kind of danger until it was
discovered that canals are a holiday amenity, and this has led to the
preservation of part of the system which might otherwise have disappeared. Associated with canals there are some superb feats of

82

Kingston Row and James Brindley Walk, Birmingham, before and after restoration of a derelict canalside. (Civic Trust Award, 1969.)

architecture, notably the aqueducts which were built to carry them over rivers and difficult pieces of ground. A number of these still survive and are splendid examples of building and engineering skill. There is one which carries the Brecknock and Abergavenny Canal over the River Usk at Brynich near Brecon in Wales, and another carries the Lancaster Canal across the River Lune near the town of Lancaster. The sight of such aqueducts helps us to appreciate the imaginative outlook of their builders—pioneers of the Industrial Revolution. Stourport in Worcestershire was created by canals, and grew up where the River Severn is joined by the Staffordshire-Worcestershire Canal. Around the Canal basin there are still eighteenth-century houses in beautiful condition to be seen. It is also worth recalling that the word 'navvy' is a shortened form of 'navigator', the name given to men who dug canals and later in the nineteenth century drove tunnels and built embankments for the railways.

With regard to roads, we can all see the tremendous programme of road-building that is going on at present. Old roads are being widened to take more traffic, and new motorways, in use and in construction, are cutting their way through the countryside. They change the appearance of the countryside considerably. Garages, service stations and cafés spring up along their length to serve the needs of road-users rather than those of local communities. The picture on the next page of a flyover overlooking houses demonstrates how the requirements of the motor-car have been given higher priority than the comfort and privacy of householders. With all this activity it is easy to overlook the fact that there was no serious road-making in this country from the time of the Romans' departure until about half-way through the nineteenth century. The usual method of making roads passable was to scrape away the mud and fill the holes with either stones or brushwood. As wheeled traffic increased during the seventeenth and eighteenth centuries the roads became worse and worse, so that water transport was the most satisfactory way of sending heavy loads. The best route by road was that which linked London, Bath and Bristol. Here a very special effort was made because Bath was the chief pleasure resort, and the other two cities were the largest in the kingdom.

A flyover overlooking houses in Western Avenue, London.

With the coming of the Industrial Revolution there was an increased need for faster travel between London and the provinces, and a more reliable means of transporting manufactured goods as well as raw materials. New roads were built by Thomas Telford (1757–1834) and John McAdam (1756–1836), on rather different principles. Telford's system was a carefully laid, packed foundation of heavy stones, and this was covered by a layer of small stones which the passing traffic would gradually settle into place. Although an improvement upon earlier methods, it was found that the top surface was too easily worn away. McAdam's method was different, and he paid a great deal of attention to drainage, believing that if both surface and foundation of the road could be kept dry by ensuring that these layers were above the level of the surrounding ground, wear and tear would be cut down, and there would be less

85

need for frequent maintenance. He avoided using a base of large stones which was quite expensive, and used small stones instead.

McAdam's theories proved more successful, and by about 1900 some ninety per cent of the roads in England and Wales had been rebuilt according to his ideas. It was a cheaper method than Telford's, and the growing use of rubber tyres cut down a good deal of wear on the roads. Solid rubber tyres had been in use from about 1850, and by the turn of the century pneumatic tyres were being made. Many modern roads are built on top of earlier ones, and it is quite possible to see during excavations the various layers

A fourteenth-century inn and oyster bar—all that remains of Manchester's Old Shambles area—stands on concrete columns while redevelopment takes place around it. The building has been raised by nearly 5 ft. to fit in with new roads.

used in the construction of roads. It is probable that a good deal of early road building is carefully preserved beneath a modern surface, so if you are lucky you will be able to see something of this.

Not all the monuments of the Industrial Revolution are as spectacular as buildings, railway stations, locomotives and the like. Chimney-pots, for example. Many varying designs are still to be seen, but as more and more buildings are centrally heated they too will disappear. Sir John Betjeman, a great lover of the past and a fighter for its survival, says that they are a vital part of the London scene, and of course they are an interesting reminder of the days when coal was the foundation upon which England's wealth was built.

Let me now indicate to you two other interesting byways which are directly related to the age of coal and iron. The first of these is the coal-hole cover which is still to be seen in city streets, and the second is the railway ticket.

When coal provided the only means of domestic heating, many houses in towns were built with cellars to which coal could be delivered through a hole in the pavement, and the covers were very interesting examples of nineteenth-century ironwork. The earliest ones date from about 1840 and were rectangular without very much in the way of design. One of these survives at Lingfield in Surrey. This shape was, however, found to be impractical because the corners too easily broke off, and circular covers were introduced instead. Many of them were very pleasantly decorated and often included the name of the maker. In fact, it is often possible to date coal-hole covers to within a few years by the maker's name, because this can often be traced in an old copy of *Kelly's Street Directory*, copies of which should be found in your local library. In Waterloo, Chelsea and Islington in London you will come across man-hole covers, and they are to be found in Liverpool, Manchester and Bath as well. They are worth looking for elsewhere, for they are a delightful reminder of a past age.

The railway ticket is something more than a memorial to the Industrial Revolution, for not only are tickets still used, but the history of the ticket illustrates also the ways in which one innovation

87

can lead to another. In the early days of rail travel, paper tickets were used, but as passengers increased in number these were found to be inconvenient and a Mr. Thomas Edmondson, a station-master in the North of England, hit upon the idea of using a card-board ticket. Not only were they simple to issue, but it was easy to keep a check upon the number issued and the amounts of money paid to the booking clerk. The first tickets were in use in 1836; and such was the popularity of the idea that it was taken up by railway companies in England and abroad, while the inventor developed machinery for printing, dating and counting tickets, and, of course, for destroying those which had been used. So we can see how the coming of railway traffic was responsible for the invention of the cardboard ticket, and the ticket in turn created a need for new machinery. Whether the railway ticket issued to you today comes from an automatic machine or from a booking clerk, the ticket itself has an interesting history which goes back for nearly one hundred and fifty years. If you are interested to pursue the subject there is an excellent little pamphlet published by the Lancashire and Cheshire Antiquarian Society, called *The Early History of the Railway Ticket*, which can be bought from Portico Library in Manchester.

Another familiar way in which the Industrial Revolution has affected our surroundings has been in the manufacture of bricks and cement. Both are so taken for granted that we could easily overlook them, but it would be hard to imagine the world as we now know it without either. Bricks are one of the oldest building materials known to man. In the early Mesopotamian, Indus and Mediterranean civilizations bricks made of sun-baked mud were in use, and the earliest brick kiln so far discovered is near Bombay in India, dating from about 2,000 B.C. It was the Romans who introduced bricks into Britain, but after they left there is no trace of a brick industry until late in the twelfth or early in the thirteenth century, when bricks were reintroduced into Britain from Flanders and Holland. By the early fifteenth century, buildings made of brick had become common. The brick industry continued to expand, and up to the 1830's bricks were made by hand, a skilled man being able to produce five thousand per day. In 1838 their manufacture was mechanized, and various technical changes were introduced; an improved kiln invented in Germany was first used in Britain in 1862, and in the 1880's further refinements became possible. These advances meant that bricks could be lighter, more uniform in quality and above all cheaper, and the industry made a great contribution to the increase in building activity which took place in London at the end of the nineteenth century.

Compared with bricks, cement has a short history, and the industry arose out of the building in the eighteenth and nineteenth centuries of canals, harbours and railways. It was in 1756 that John Smeaton, who was building the Eddystone Lighthouse, needed a cement that would set almost immediately under water. His experiments were successful and he commented that he had made 'a cement that would equal the best merchantable Portland stone in solidity and durability'. Further improvements in cement-making took place and in 1824 Joseph Aspdin, a Leeds bricklayer, was granted a patent for what he described as 'Portland Cement'. The development of cement production was so rapid that in addition to its extensive use in building, over half a million tons of cement were exported each year by the late 1880's.

The picture on the jacket of a gas-lighter still at work in the London of the 1970's is a reminder that up to the eighteenth century domestic lighting relied upon an open fire, oil lamps and candles. It was William Murdoch who first used coal gas commercially as a means of lighting. He was employed by the firm of engineers Boulton and Watt, of Soho near Birmingham, and it was here that Murdoch carried out his experiments. By 1803 permanent gas lighting was installed at the Boulton and Watt works, and shortly afterwards the firm began to manufacture apparatus for making, storing and purifying gas for use in factories. Between 1805 and 1807 Murdoch erected a gas-making plant at the cotton mill of Phillips and Lee in Salford. The cost of lighting the mill was £600 a year, while for candles to provide the same light the bill would have been £2,000.

Clearly this saving indicated a profitable field of investment, and the use of gas for street lighting was soon under consideration. In

1810 the Gas Light and Coke Company secured through an Act of Parliament the right to supply gas in the cities of London and Westminster, Southwark and the adjoining parishes and suburbs. From this time onwards the gas industry expanded tremendously.

One of the oddest things which helped its expansion in the years of depression after the war against Napoleon had ended in 1815 was the availability of large Government stocks of surplus musket barrels, at £13 to £17 per ton, which were taken into use as pipes; and at the same time old cannons were used as lamp-posts. After gas for lighting, gas for cooking was developed. This began in around 1824 and although progress was much slower than it had been in the case of lighting, efficient gas cooking stoves were made both in Ipswich and in Liverpool in 1850.

From the late 1870's electric lighting was a competitor but the invention of the gas mantle meant that the illuminating power of gas was doubled, so that this method of lighting not only held its ground against its rival, but also enabled it to extend its markets. Penny-in-the-slot meters first appeared in large numbers in 1889, and this invention by which gas was paid for as it was consumed meant that gas could now be used by those people who could not afford to pay quarterly bills.

Finally, a feature of the modern

An early mainland letter box made by John M. Butt & Co. of Gloucester, *circa* 1853. Location: Barnes Cross, Bishop's Caundle, Dorset. (By courtesy of the Post Office.)

landscape, of which there are more than 95,000 examples to be seen—the letter box. We take it for granted, of course; but it has an interesting history, and certainly not all the examples you will see are modern. Many of the earlier ones will have the royal cipher VR, showing that they were erected between 1837 and 1901.

Although posting boxes were in use in Paris in 1653, the first one in England was an iron box in the wall at Wakefield Post Office in 1809. In 1840 the penny post was introduced, and in 1851 Anthony Trollope the novelist, who worked for the Post Office, recommended the use of roadside posting boxes in the Channel Islands. In the following year pillar-boxes were introduced in St. Helier, Jersey, and three years later they made their appearance in London. In 1858 wall boxes were introduced, and thirteen years afterwards— in 1871—enamelled 'Hours of collection' notices came generally into use.

In 1964 there took place 'The Pillar-Box Treasure Hunt'. Readers of the *Post Office Magazine* were asked to report any old pillar-boxes, and the results were surprising—many boxes of which the Post Office had no records were 'discovered', and all these are recorded in a charming book, *The Letter Box* (Centaur Press, 1969), by J. Y. Farrugia, who was incidentally the originator of the hunt. You should certainly consult this book if the subject appeals to you.

I hope these examples—bricks, cement, gas and post-boxes—will suggest to you fresh ways of looking for the history which underlies so much of our landscape and so much in our lives which we take for granted. If you are interested to follow up these aspects of the Industrial Revolution you should look at a copy of *People and Industries* by W. H. Chaloner (Frank Cass & Co. Ltd., 1963). About half this book is taken up with the lives of some of the pioneers of technical change, and the remainder with an account of those industries which are closely connected with our daily lives, such as paper, and the canning of food. It is at this point, when we consider the lives of men and women, that local history and social history become one. If natural and man-made landscapes in history are to have reality for us, they must be peopled by inhabitants in our imaginations as they once were in fact.

8   Battles and Battlefields

On looking at the English countryside it is difficult to believe that it has ever been touched by war. Even the castles and the ruins of castles have today an air of serenity and peace. It is easy to forget that the Roman roads were built by an invader so that his armies could move through the country. It is, of course, true that our countryside has not been scarred by warfare to the same extent as, say, the plains of Flanders in Belgium, which have earned the nickname 'the cock-pit of Europe'. The last successful invasion of our shores was undertaken by the Normans over nine hundred years ago, and we can justifiably conclude that our immunity from invasions is due partly to the fact that we are an island and partly to the existence of the Navy dating back at least to the reign of King John.

Nonetheless, battles have been fought here, and this is an aspect of the past where reconstruction is often possible. Before the Norman Conquest many battles were fought between warring tribes who inhabited these islands and between the Britons and the Romans. There was a great battle against a Roman army at Maiden Castle; but the only sites we can be really sure about are those of battles which were fought after 1066. Since this Norman invasion, all the major battles have been fought either against the Scots or in a time of civil strife.

Just as the geographical fact of our being an island is to a great extent responsible for our freedom from foreign invasion, so the geographical pattern of Great Britain has influenced the conduct of the wars which have been fought here. Most of the big battles have taken place in the Midlands, rather than in the North which is more hilly. In the wars which were fought over a long period against the Welsh and against the Scots, the lie of the land played an important part. The River Severn and its valley is a natural frontier between England and Wales, and the mountains formed a barrier to invasion: not only would it be difficult to cross them in the face of a determined enemy, but the invading army would be hard put to it to find enough to eat. In the past, armies lived off the land through which they were passing, and in these barren mountains there was little to be had.

So far as Scotland was concerned the River Forth was a considerable barrier. For centuries Stirling commanded the only bridge, and the castle there had to be taken if the Highlands were to be occupied. Farther south the Pennines gave little choice of invasion routes into Scotland or from Scotland into England— there were two, an eastern route and a western one. An army of foot-soldiers, horsemen and guns could travel only by one or the other of these. Cromwell going north in 1650 went east of the Pennines; Bonnie Prince Charlie coming south in 1745 chose the western route.

Rivers have played some part in shaping military campaigns. The Severn Valley was the scene of several battles, at Shrewsbury, Tewkesbury, Evesham and Worcester. Similarly the River Trent— Newark was the scene of a Royalist victory in 1644, and it was here that the Great North Road crossed the river.

Any battle is a tremendous event to those who take part in it. For a whole variety of reasons men will risk death or mutilation, sometimes for a cause they barely understand. They are often inspired to perform acts of rare courage and self-sacrifice. Many battles are key points in history, for they take place as the climax of events in which differences of opinion or policy grow so acute that it is felt at the time that they can only be resolved by fighting.

Even, however, without detailed knowledge of the background to a specific battle, you will find that few landscapes are so full of atmosphere as a battlefield. To visit Naseby, for example, on a late summer afternoon is a strangely moving experience, and it takes no great effort of the imagination to see Cromwell's Ironsides charging and routing Prince Rupert's cavalry, to hear the thunder of their hoofs, the cries of soldiers and the crackle of musket fire. Not all battlefields have remained unchanged as this one has, and in this chapter I shall provide a list of some of the more important sites; but first, here is a list of books which provide useful background reading, and the plans of various battles:

David Scott Daniell, *Battles and Battlefields*, Batsford, 1961. This is a good general introduction with pictures, family trees and plans of individual battles.

A. H. Burne, *The Battlefields of England* and *More Battlefields of England*, Methuen, 1951 and 1952.

Peter Young and John Adair, *Hastings to Culloden, Battlefields in Britain*, Bell, 1964.

These three books should be consulted for individual battles, and the campaigns leading up to them.

A. H. Burne and Peter Young, *The Great Civil War, a Military History of the First Civil War 1642–1646*, Eyre and Spottiswoode, 1959. An excellent account of the struggle between King and Parliament. The plans of individual battles are extremely clear.

C. N. Barclay, *Battle 1066*, Dent, 1966.

I. C. Taylor, *Culloden. A Guidebook to the Battlefield with the Story of the Battle, the Events leading to it, and the Aftermath*, National Trust for Scotland, 1965.

The first of these is a short book and the second a pamphlet. Each, as the titles suggest, deals with a specific engagement. Both of these publications are illustrated with pictures and maps and from each one it is possible to gain a very clear idea of what the battle was like, what led up to it and what its consequences were. Maps from these publications are reproduced in this chapter.

There are also two volumes on battlefields in the 'Discovering' books series referred to on page 109. These are *Discovering Battlefields in Northern England and Scotland* and *Discovering Battlefields in Southern England* by John Kinross.

Finally, two older books which may not be easy to come across. If you ask at your local library, they may be able to locate copies which you can borrow.

C. R. B. Barrett, *Battles and Battlefields in England*, London, 1896. This is rather a long book, but the author's plans and drawings give it an unusual charm, and on some of the less important battles and skirmishes it is very informative.

Hillaire Belloc, *Warfare in England*, Williams and Norgate, no date (probably about 1912). Despite the fact that it was published so long ago, this is a bright and freshly written book. The author was an enthusiast and is able to communicate his enthusiasm to the reader of today.

With these titles I have touched upon some of the most useful background books. Undoubtedly if you are interested you will find others, especially if you live near the place where a battle was fought in the past, for it is more than likely that someone will have written about it.

Here in chronological order is a list of some important battlefields which are to be seen in England and Scotland with brief reminders of the circumstances of the battles themselves.

Hastings, 1066
A crucial moment in our history. Harold, the Saxon King, faced the invading army of Duke William of Normandy, who became King William I.

Battle is a small town about $6\frac{3}{4}$ miles north-west of Hastings on the A21 at the junction with the B2092. If you look at the map showing the battle area in 1966, and compare it with the one showing the country as it was nine hundred years ago when the Saxons fought the Normans (pp. 98 and 97), you will see that a number of changes have taken place. Caldbec Hill is the best starting point; other places from which the field can be looked at are numbered on the more up-to-date of the two maps. In the grounds of Battle Abbey is the high altar (HA on the map) which marks the position

95

of Harold's headquarters during the battle. If you walk down to the railway bridge on the main road and look from there towards Senlac Hill, you can see the position of the English army very much as the Normans must have seen it.

Lewes, 1264
Simon de Montfort defeated King Henry III.

Lewes is eight miles north-east of Brighton. The road to the race-course is where most of the fighting took place.

Evesham, 1265
The protagonists here were again Simon de Montfort and the Royalist army, this time led by Prince Edward. Simon de Montfort was killed, and Henry III was restored to power.

Evesham is fifteen miles south-east of Worcester. North of the town at the junction of the A435 and the B4084 roads is the best place from which to see the battlefield.

Bannockburn, 1314
Edward II fought here against the Scots under Robert the Bruce, and failed to conquer them.

The battle took place one mile south-east of Stirling, and the scene of the fiercest fighting was probably where the railway line crosses the A905 road.

St. Albans, first battle 1455, second battle 1461
In the first of these battles the opposing armies were commanded by Henry VI and Richard, Duke of York. This event precipitated the Wars of the Roses, and in the second battle here the Duke of Somerset triumphantly led the Lancastrian army against the Earl of Warwick, the Yorkist leader.

The battlefields are best seen from the top of the bell tower. A small charge is made for admission but this is the only way to see the ground. There is a plaque on the wall of the National Westminster Bank and the position of Key field is marked by a street name; and there are a number of relics from the two battlefields in the local museum. To see what the armour of the period looked like, you should look at the brass of Sir Antony de Grey in the Abbey.

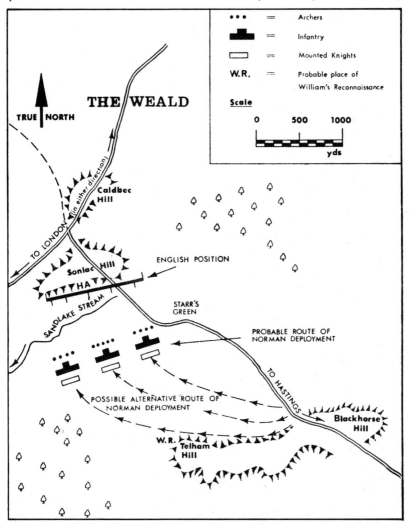

• • •	=	Archers
▄▄▟▄▄	=	Infantry
▭	=	Mounted Knights
W.R.	=	Probable place of William's Reconnaissance

The Battle of Hastings. A map of the battle area as it was in 1066.

97

Towton, 1461
The result of the St. Albans battle was speedily reversed here, and
the Duke of Somerset fled with the Lancastrian army from the
Yorkists.

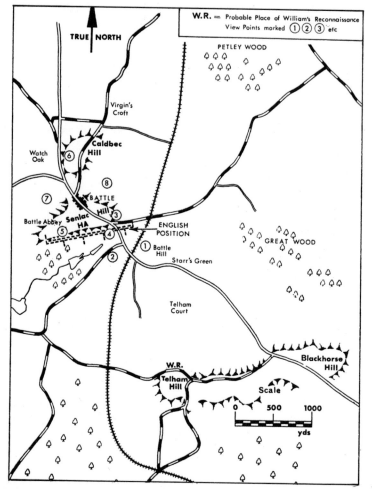

The Battle of Hastings. A map of the battle area drawn in 1966. The numbers in
circles indicate the best positions *on the ground* from which the battlefield may be
seen today.

Between York and Leeds the B3679 road cuts the battlefield in two. Close by, in Saxton parish churchyard, there is the tomb of Lord Dacre who fought in the battle.

Tewkesbury, 1471
Another battle of the Wars of the Roses. The forces of Margaret of Anjou, Henry VI's Queen, were routed by the Yorkists under Edward IV.

The site of the battle is south-east of the Abbey, but the ground has changed greatly and it is hard to explore the positions of the opposing armies.

Bosworth, 1485
This was the battle in which Henry Tudor defeated Richard III, and it concluded the Wars of the Roses. Lord Stanley placed King Richard's crown on Henry Tudor's head; and thus the Tudor dynasty began.

Ambien Hill, about fourteen miles east of Leicester by road, is the best place from which to see the battlefield. A monument, King Richard's Well, was erected in 1813 and marks the scene of the fighting.

Flodden, 1513
One of the battles fought against the Scots. An interesting feature was that the British victory could be attributed to their combination of field artillery, archers and infantry.

Two miles south-east of Coldstream lies Branxton where the fighting took place. A monument commemorating the battle lies five hundred yards or so south-west of the village.

The following five were all battles of the English Civil War. Naseby was the scene of the decisive battle, and the defeat of the Royalists meant that the Stuart cause was doomed. Although the war dragged on for a few more years this was the last major battle, and it represented a triumph for Cromwell's New Model Army.

99

Edgehill, 1642

The battlefield, which lies to the west of the A41 road from Warwick to Banbury, is on land controlled by the War Department. On the ridge by Edge Hill itself, however, there is the Castle Inn and from its ornamental tower it is possible to see the battlefield as a whole.

Newbury, first battle 1643

At The Gun public house on the A343 from Newbury towards Andover, there is a monument to Lord Falkland who died fighting on the Royalist side. There are some relics in the town museum.

Marston Moor, 1644

The battlefield is on the B1224 road about six miles west of York. Although a cottage in the near-by village of Tockwith, where it is said that Oliver Cromwell had a wound tended, was destroyed by a bomb during the Second World War, the site of the battle looks now very much as it did in 1644. An obelisk stands on the spot where there was much fighting.

Newbury, second battle 1644

The site of the battlefield is north of the town, and it can best be viewed from Donnington Castle, whose ruins lie about half a mile to the west of the A34 road to Oxford, some one and a half miles from Newbury. There are some relics in the town museum.

Naseby, 1645

Naseby can best be reached by the B3046 from Market Harborough. The battlefield, very little changed, is on the road from Naseby to Tockwith. There is a Naseby obelisk which was erected in 1825, but it is a mile from where the fighting took place. A monument recently erected by the Cromwell Association roughly indicates the position of the right wing of the army at the beginning of the action. There are several battle relics in the village church.

Dunbar, 1650

Cromwell defeated the Scots decisively, and this battle culminated in the surrender of Edinburgh Castle.

The battlefield, little altered, is easily reached from the main A1
at Dunbar to Cockburnspath Road.

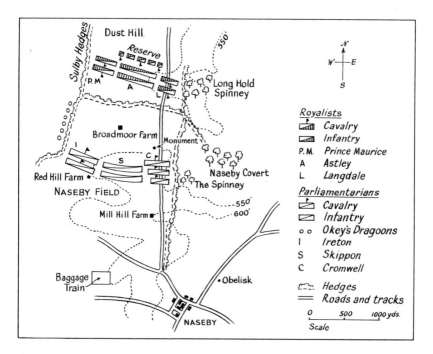

The Battle of Naseby, 1645. (Prince Maurice was Prince Rupert's brother.)

Worcester, 1651
Another defeat of the Royalist forces under Charles II. Cromwell
described this battle as 'the crowning mercy', and after this the
Royalists never again put an army into the field against him.

The Commandery, an early seventeenth-century house which was
the Royalist headquarters, can still be seen, and it was from the
Cathedral that the King looked over the battlefield. At near-by
Powick there are the marks of musket balls on the south wall of the
church tower, and there are repairs to an arch of the old brick
bridge. There had been a skirmish in the village nine years earlier,

when Prince Rupert put some Roundhead cavalry to flight.

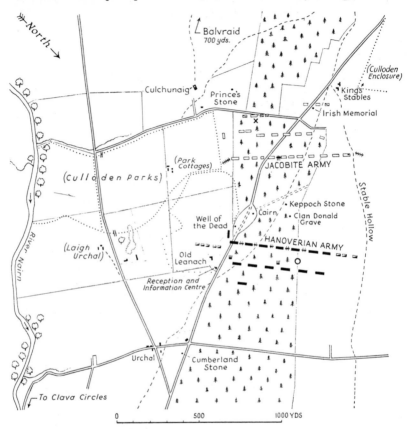

The Battle of Culloden, 1746. A map of the battlefield today.

Sedgemoor, 1685

The claimant, the Duke of Monmouth, was decisively defeated by the army of James II. The battle was followed by the so-called 'Bloody Assizes', in which Judge Jeffreys sentenced many of the rebel troops to death or transportation. This was the last battle fought on English soil. On the battlefield there is a memorial with the following inscription: 'To the Glory of God, and in memory of all those, who, doing the right as they saw it, fell in the battle of Sedgemoor, 6th July, 1685, and lie buried in this field, or who, for their share in the fight, suffered death, punishment or transportation, PRO PATRIA.'

The battlefield is about three miles south of Bridgwater on the A372, and still looks very much as it must have done when the action took place. At Chedzoy near by one can still see the place where the Royalist soldiers sharpened their swords before the battle.

Culloden, 1746

The last battle fought in the British Isles. The British army under the Duke of Cumberland defeated the Jacobite army under Prince Charles Edward Stuart, the Young Pretender.

About seven miles east of Inverness the battlefield can be reached by the B9006 road. The area of the fighting is now mostly covered by trees, but the cairn which marks the burial-place of those killed is in a clearing. The National Trust for Scotland is now responsible for the site.

This list is by no means complete, but it does contain the most important engagements which took place over a period of about seven hundred years. Culloden was the last battle to be fought on British soil. The Battle of Hastings was by no means the first; but we have few precise details of sites, or of the opposing forces in these earlier actions. Nor do we know exactly *when* they took place, so that while we can be sure that the life of early man in these islands was often made turbulent by war, we cannot say more than this. There are virtually no facts to go on.

9 How to form a Local-History Reference Collection

In this chapter I want to say something about a very important element in looking for the past. This is the formation of your own collection of reference material which will reflect all that you have found most interesting in your search. The formation of such a collection can be very enjoyable, and need be neither so difficult nor so expensive as you might think. Of course some books are highly priced, and some are not only expensive but also very hard to find, but it is always worth while looking in second-hand book-shops, and you may, if you are lucky, come across old prints on stalls in open-air markets. The kind of reference collection which I have in mind does not really present too many difficulties, and will cost very little.

All kinds of pamphlets and guide-books are published. Some may cost you up to about 30p, others may cost even less, and a few are to be had free. Let me, then, begin by giving you some idea of the sort of thing that you might look for.

Some very useful, attractive and inexpensive publications are issued by the Government publishers, Her Majesty's Stationery Office. Amongst them is a twelve-page leaflet called *Maiden Castle Dorset* by Sir Mortimer Wheeler. This provides a brief account of the earthworks described in Chapter Two, together with a very clearly drawn plan. Then there is Professor Chambers' guide *Laxton, the Last English Open Field Village*, forty-four pages, splendidly illustrated with photographs, maps and plans. This village, which was mentioned in an earlier chapter, is a very important one, and Professor Chambers has written a fascinating account of this survival from the Middle Ages. An even earlier England is recalled in Leonard Cottrell's *The Roman Forts of the Saxon Shore*. This forty-page survey describes the fortifications which stretched round the south-eastern coast from Brancaster to Portchester, and there are some admirable photographs and plans which vividly recreate these remains of Roman Britain.

Museum handbooks are another valuable aid to the local historian. Let me mention two in particular. The Inland Water-ways' canal museum at Stoke Bruerne in Northamptonshire publishes an illustrated handbook which is well worth having, although it is of course no substitute for actually visiting this fascinating museum. Then, too, there is the guide to the Welsh Folk Museum at St. Fagan's. This handbook, which contains some very good illustrations, is useful, but again it is no substitute for a visit to this museum where the past has literally been re-created.

Other museum handbooks—and I mention only a few of the many which are published—include the one for the Anne of Cleves House Museum at Southover, Lewes in Sussex. The house itself was built in about 1500 and today it houses a most interesting and unusual collection. There are some excellent pieces of Sussex ironwork, old furniture and dresses. This could easily sound very dull, but if we are to build up a picture of how people lived in the past it is necessary to see how they lived at home, the clothes they wore and the furniture they used. One of the everyday things to be seen there is a shepherd's umbrella; these are very scarce indeed, and the sight of this one, together with the shepherd's crook and smock, remind us of a way of life on the South Downs that has long since vanished.

The handbook of the Geffrye Museum, London, is also worth having, for it contains illustrations of the period room in the museum itself with its collection of furniture and fittings. Most museums in fact publish guides to their exhibitions, and nearly all of them are worth buying and keeping.

Official guides, too, should form part of your collection of reference material, and they can usually be had free of charge, or for a few pence, if you inquire at the Town Hall. Most of these guide-books will contain some historical notes, and I have not yet seen one that does not include a map. The guide to Dorchester is an interesting one. Let me mention one that is particularly useful from the historical point of view. This is the official guide to Bridgwater in Somerset, which provides a very good account, with illustrations, of the town as it is today, together with its history, also illustrated. Guides like this can be a very valuable aid to the local historian. You should certainly be aware of them, and such official publications are usually the easiest to come by.

Many of the London Boroughs are becoming increasingly aware of their history, and this is reflected in the quality of some of their publications. Hackney is one of these. There is *A Short History of the London Borough of Hackney*, a sixteen-page illustrated booklet; and this, with their *Why Mare Street? A Short Index of Street Names*, is of especial interest because street names can so often give a clue to history of quite an unexpected sort. There is in Hackney a Loddiges Road; it is named after the Loddiges family who were gardeners in the area from 1771, and it was they who introduced rhubarb and rhododendrons into this country. The London Borough of Tower Hamlets, too, issues free of charge a twelve-page booklet called *Finding Out About Local History*, which includes a number of illustrations.

Sheffield City Libraries have produced a number of leaflets on aspects of local history, dealing with such subjects as railways, Mary Queen of Scots, hospitals, water-mills, and printing. You will also find that Essex Record Office has issued some splendidly illustrated brochures, and one of them, *The Face of Essex*, provides in forty-two plates a splendid view of how man's imprint upon the country has changed from prehistoric times to the present. This is not the only booklet published by Essex Record Office, whose productions also include *Essex Homes*, *Victorian Essex*, and a number of other titles.

The list of libraries and Record Offices issuing local material could be extended, and you should see what is available in your own neighbourhood.

Quite apart from the guides published by local authorities, it is always worth inquiring, even in small towns and villages, whether anybody has written a pamphlet about the area. At Puddletown in Dorset, for example, copies of a history of the town written by the Vicar, the Reverend O. D. Harvey, were on sale in the church some years ago.

Local historical societies occasionally publish books which are very worth while, and often cheap to buy. In the Midlands, there is a Peak District Mines Historical Society, whose well-illustrated book *Local Mining in the Peak District* is a guide to this industry which has long since disappeared. Published at Bakewell in 1968, it contains diagrams, photographs and maps. Most interesting of all, perhaps, there is a glossary of some of the commonest words which are peculiar to the Derbyshire lead-mining area. Although words are not visible in the sense that relics of, say, Derbyshire mining or an old church can be called visible, language can provide important clues to life in the past. This is particularly true of place-names, but can also apply to both words and phrases which have now disappeared. For this reason I think the glossary at the end of this booklet is indispensable. There may well be a local-history group of some kind where you live, and you will be able to find out whether they have published anything.

Churches, as we have seen, are always worth visiting, and in many of them pamphlet histories of the church can be bought for a few pence. Such publications vary a great deal. Among the best I have seen are *The Church of St. Michael and All Angels Ledbury*, and *By the Banks of the Ouse*, a very pleasantly produced booklet about the parish church at Olney in Buckinghamshire. Amongst the London churches, *The Church of St. Margaret Pattens Eastcheap* has its history presented with a reproduction from an old print. The author, Gordon Huelin, has also written a small book about the thirty-five churches in the City of London which were not rebuilt after the Great Fire of 1666 (*The Pre-Fire City Churches*). In most cases the site has been built over. All Hallows in Honey Lane, for example, stood north of Cheapside, and today the Sun Life office stands in its place. In Oat Lane, beside Pewterers' Hall, there is a garden with some tombstones; this is the churchyard of St. Mary Staining, a church which was first mentioned in 1189. On the corner of Old Jewry there is a City Corporation plaque marking the site of St. Mary Colechurch. Peter, the chaplain of St. Mary Colechurch in 1171, was the builder of Old London Bridge. The tracing of these old churches is fascinating, and calls to mind a past when the life of London was centred in the City, and it was not, as it is today, the commercial heart of the capital.

. . .

There are other inexpensive publications which ought to find a place in your collection. London Transport issue a number of leaflets which are free. *Windmills in and Around London* is unusual. Who would have thought that there is a mill built in 1816 in Brixton, carefully restored by the Greater London Council? It can be seen in an open space appropriately called Windmill Gardens. Then, too, there are leaflets dealing with buildings designed by Christopher Wren and John Nash. The first is delightfully illustrated, and the second has a detailed map showing just where Nash buildings are to be seen. If you are keen on museums, then you should certainly have their *Museums and Art Galleries in and near London*, an extremely useful little book which not only tells you where the museums are, but also when they open and how to reach them. Did you know, for example, that there is a National Postal Museum in King Edward Street, E.C.1? It is open from Monday to Friday from 10 am to 4.30 pm, on Saturday from 10 am to 4 pm. For a few pence you can buy their *London's Industrial Archaeology*, a fascinating booklet which includes details of how to see such relics as the nineteenth-century potteries of Holland Park. If you turn right outside the station, then right again into Portland Road, and bear left up Pottery Lane, you are in the centre of an area which used to be known for its yellow clay which was used for bricks and pottery. At the end of Pottery Lane stands a kiln, a physical reminder of days when this area was famous for its pottery—and also for its crime and its slums.

For one final selection from London Transport's leaflets, let me recommend *Roundabout*. This is described as 'A selection of items of curiosity and interest', and it includes some fascinating suggestions for visits and unexpected items of information. No guarantee can be given about the availability of these publications—some may go out of print, while others are always being added.

For 30p each you can buy *Historic Houses, Castles and Gardens* and *Museums and Galleries in Great Britain and Ireland* (each published annually by ABC Travel Guides Ltd). These illustrated guides list hundreds of properties and museums in Great Britain and Ireland

Dobson's Mill, a five-sail windmill built in 1833 at Burgh-le-Marsh, Lincolnshire, was bought by Lindsey County Council and has been completely restored, with the accompanying farm dray, by boys of the Morris Secondary School, Skegness.

and give full details of opening times and admission charges.

Lastly, there are the 'Discovering' books. These are moderately priced and because they all measure $7'' \times 4\frac{1}{2}''$ they will fit easily into your pocket. Shire Publications, who issue these books, say that they are designed as 'an aid to the reader to enjoy and understand—in fact to discover—his surroundings'. I have already mentioned John Camp's *Discovering London Railway Stations* and John Kinross's *Discovering Battlefields*. Other subjects covered include windmills, brasses, wayside graves, hill figures, Gloucestershire, wall paintings, inn signs—there are in fact over eighty titles in the series. The two books which are, I think, especially valuable for the local historian are *Discovering Towns* by John Haddon, and *Discovering This Old House* by David Iredale. The first is an excellent introduction to looking at towns with an inquisitive eye. It is very well illustrated, and if you have it with you when you walk through a town, even if it is well known to you, you will see roads, buildings and other things in a new and more interesting light. The other book says a good deal that is very helpful about old houses, and how we can learn something about them. It is also well illustrated, and adds fresh pleasure and knowledge to the pursuit of the past.

There are, of course, many other sources which you will readily discover for yourselves. I have mentioned only a few amongst a large number of books, pamphlets and leaflets which may be of use to you. The quantity of material which you can collect quite easily and cheaply, together with its variety of size and shape, does create a problem—or, rather, two problems which are related, that of storage, and that of deciding what you want in your own collection.

The main guiding line for a collector is *be selective*. It is no use at all attempting to collect everything; but however selective you are, it is quite possible that you may have a wide range of material. Books are no problem for they will live happily on a shelf. Pamphlets and leaflets are more difficult to deal with, because it is so easy just to keep them in an untidy heap. This not only makes it very difficult for you to locate a particular item when you want it, but may also cause damage to publications which are quite fragile. An inexpensive and satisfactory method of storage is to obtain a number of cardboard boxes with lids, arrange your collection according to the subjects, and keep each section, or if they are very small, two or three sections, in its own box. On the outside of each box paste a list of its contents; then, providing you always replace an item in its right place when you have used it, the task of finding a specific title will be greatly simplified. You will have a great deal of pleasure in assembling your own local-history reference collection, and it will also be extremely useful and personal to you.

10   Voices from the Past

As we saw in the opening chapter, the lives of ordinary people in the past are of great interest to the local historian. No landscape, whether in town or country, of whatever century, can begin to live in our imagination unless it is inhabited by men and women going about their daily affairs whose concern with the problems of everyday living was in many ways very similar to our own.

So far as the remote past is concerned we have little to go on, but the monuments of prehistory are sometimes so striking—Maiden Castle, for example, or the Iron Age village at Chysauster in Cornwall—that no tremendous effort of the imagination is needed to see them peopled with thriving communities. Similarly, the Roman Wall in the North of England reminds us of the soldiers who formed its garrison. In the same way, cathedrals such as those at Lincoln or Hereford provide us with insight into the medieval world.

Strangely enough it is the more recent past which seems more distant. This is partly because only recently have we thought seriously about preserving something at least of the heritage of the last two or three centuries, and partly because in the flurry of rebuilding and redevelopment which has taken place since the end of the Second World War, we have become used to seeing much of the past that was connected with ordinary men and women—houses, cottages, railways, machinery and so on—bulldozed away to make space for office blocks, skyscraper flats, housing estates and the like. It is inevitable in a crowded island life like ours that in order to rebuild and to develop, any existing structures have to be destroyed first; but it is worth recalling that during the eighteenth century much of the building took place in what was then countryside. Listen to what one man said about it:

'The parish of Clerkenwell was very different when I first visited it in

1787 to what it is at the time of writing this paragraph in 1850. The church, which now stands at the junction of the Close and the Green, was not then erected; but in its place was the church of the old Monastic Priory, with parts of the Cloisters &c. Spa Fields, from the south end of Rosoman Street to Pentonville and from St. John-Street Road to the Bagnigge-Wells Road were really fields devoted to the pasturage of cows, and to a forest of elm trees; not standing and adorned with foliage in the summer, but lying on the ground to the southward of New River Head; being destined to convey water in their hollow trunks to the northern and western parts of London in combination with similar pipes laid under the roadways of the streets.'

John Britton, who wrote this, was not a Londoner, so what he saw must have made a considerable impact upon him. Further on in the passage quoted he says that in 1801 there were 3,427 houses in Clerkenwell and in 1841, 7,242.

Britton's recollections of London were printed in his autobiography. He had been born in Wiltshire in 1771 of very poor parents, and what he writes about his childhood in the village of Kington provides a view of village life at the end of the eighteenth century. He tells us that the roads from the village which led to the turnpikes were little more than tracks used mostly by wagons and carts which, together with the horses, wore great ruts in them. The most frequent visitor to the village was a clothier, bringing wool for the village women to spin for the weaver's loom, and occasionally a quack doctor came. His description of the village and the house where he was born is remarkably clear:

'I believe nearly the whole of my time, from my thirteenth to my sixteenth year (that is, from 1784–1787) was spent in my native village; either in idle play, or in thus assisting my parents in their daily labours. My clearest recollections of Kington, and of our own rustic dwelling, refer therefore to this period. The houses of the village were placed mostly on the sides of a wide street, which extends nearly a mile in length. To the east there were, however, not more than sixteen in the whole extent, most of which were insulated, and at considerable distances from their "next door neighbours". On the west side there was a row, either attached, or with short spaces between them. Among these were a

112

slaughter-house, a tailor's and two other shops, a public house, a malt house and a group of twelve dwellings called "Alderman Lyte's Alms-Houses". A carpenter's, two blacksmiths', six farm-houses, the Squire's and the Parsonage, with some other tenements, made up the remainder of the village. A curate, with a small stipend, officiated weekly at the church; and after the deaths of Lady Forester and "Madam White", who had occupied the "Great House" in my infancy, it was shut up and deserted. The cottages and shops were of the humblest and poorest kind. With walls of rough undressed stone and mortar, thatched roofs, stone slabs from the quarries, or the bare earth for the floor, windows of varied forms and sizes, many of them papered or boarded, or with broken glass, it may be concluded that they were not calculated to form comfortable homes for labouring men on their return from a hard day's work. The house in which I was born . . . presented rather a better aspect than most of its neighbours; as the whole of the walls were "rough cast", having a coarse pebbly surface, which was white-washed. The roof was covered with successive layers of thatch, and the external and internal finishing was rude and simple. One room "served for kitchen and parlour and hall". It was about fourteen feet square by six feet and a half high; with a large beam beneath the ceiling, attached to which was a bacon-rack, which served to hold two flitches, with a gun, sticks, whips and other articles. The floor consisted of irregular slabs of stone, not more than an inch in thickness.'

The Autobiography of John Britton, FSA, Part I,
1850, pages 55, 61.

Autobiographies of this kind are often genuine 'voices from the past' for they describe a world which has long since vanished. John de Fraine, for example, born at Aylesbury, Buckinghamshire, in 1838, had a very clear recollection of some of the 'characters' of his town whom he knew when he was a child:

'The characters and oddities of my native town were, in these boyish days quite a source of wonderment to me, and my father's witty stories about them come fresh to my memory today, and fill me with delight. Sally Stopps who sold the "twists and jibbers" and sweets at which I looked so wistfully, and which got so few; Betty Godding, who although she was a woman, was the "postman", and delivered letters every morning all through the place; Jimmy Tucker the sweep, and Towerton the gravedigger, and Taylor the crier, and Jacob Tight the noisy drover who had the reputation of knowing "everything but what a fool he was." '

The Life of John de Fraine, 1900, p. 14.

This kind of recollection is matched by Thomas Cooper's mention of seeing as a child in Gainsborough, Lincolnshire, sailors returning from the war in 1815 or 16. He talks of:

'The return of sailors from service in the navy to their wives and families and their stories of the press-gang, and life on board "men-of-war" as the huge ships were called; the coming home of soldiers also from the war. . . .'

The Life of Thomas Cooper written by himself, London, 1872, p. 30.

Such a reference is brief, but it does at least show the kind of thing which remained in Cooper's memory for more than half a century. Similar memories are to be found in William Lovett's autobiography. His birthplace was Newlyn, Cornwall, and he recalled that in 1803 a ship carrying a cargo of raisins was wrecked on the coast, and as a result there was a plentiful supply of raisins in the town. He too, like Cooper, mentions the press-gang and fishermen who had hidden in cornfields to avoid being taken for the Navy, being ridden down by soldiers on horseback.

Details of this kind provide us with the flavour of the times, and we can sense, however briefly and indistinctly, some of the concerns of men and women. As a very distinguished local historian, Professor W. G. Hoskins, has told the writer, 'It's no good studying only houses, you must think of the people who lived in them'.

From an earlier period, we can catch a glimpse of a boy, Samuel Hutton, born in Derby in 1733. His childhood was far from happy:

'My father's table was not well provided at his lodgings. On Sunday it produced a small piece of boiled beef; on the Monday, the remains of it cold; and on the five following days oatmeal hasty pudding. Potatoes were not then known as common food. The breakfasts were of bread and milk; the suppers of bread and cheese.

'I slept on a bag of chaff thrown under the stairs and my only covering was an old ragged petticoat. I was chidden and beaten by the woman in whose house we lodged; I was kicked and cuffed by her sons; and I was whipped by my father, who was frequently heard to say that he wished somebody would take me off his hands. This treatment made me stubborn. I knew I had no friend, and I was often invincibly silent when I was asked a question.

'At seven years of age, I was set to work in the silk mills, where I toiled from five o'clock in the morning till seven at night for the weekly sum of one shilling. This paid for my board and lodging, and rendered me independent of my father except for the clothes I wore.'

Llewellyn Jewitt, F.S.A., *The Life of William Hutton and the History of the Hutton Family*, London, n.d., p. 60.

Such examples from the eighteenth century are rare, and one is tempted to wonder whether William Tomkins led this kind of life . . . at all events it adds some colour to our picture of what eighteenth-century life was like. Samuel Hutton became a soldier and fought at the battle of Minden, where he was taken prisoner by the French.

Almost one hundred years after Samuel Hutton, James Dunn was born in a village south of Charnley Forest in Leicestershire. His father, an engineer, became a drunkard, and the family was reduced to poverty. As he says:

'My school days—for the greater part, at least—were hard times for me. Most days I felt the pangs of hunger; our usual food consisted of gruel, potatoes and bread with occasionally a little bacon—and but a scant supply of that. This kind of daily living was not very helpful or stimulating to a boy in his endeavour to master his lessons. I persevered however, and was helped by the schoolmaster, the kind clergyman of the village, and private tutor to his family. My poor mother plied her needle almost night and day—for she was skilful at making certain garments—and I helped as best I could before and after school hours. I well remember how eagerly I would run on an errand, however far it was, to earn a few coppers to help procure our daily food. Sometimes it was a journey of a few miles, and if it should be to the house of a gentleman or a generous farmer, I would get a good meal, which was eagerly accepted. I also helped, as well as I was able, in the harvest time, and

115

would be up early enough week-day mornings to call men up, in time for them to be at their work by 6 o'clock. I assisted my "shoemaker" schoolmaster, who was also parish clerk, grave digger, choir master, overseer, and in fact filled almost every post in the village. Thus, in a variety of ways I used often to get food, and sometimes pence to help the home-board.'

Later, when he was a little older than Hutton, he went off to work in a coal-mine:

'I shall never forget my mother preparing my little garments for the "mine". A flannel shirt, with wide trousers, a cap, a smock-frock—all made of flannel—while the shoemaker supplied the usual heavy nailed shoes. The distance from home to the pits was about two miles. I had to have my breakfast of gruel etc., before five o'clock, so as to be at the pithead by six.

'My wages were at the rate of tenpence a day, but as the colliers seldom worked more than half-days, my week's wages rarely came to more than two shillings and sixpence.'

From Coal Mine Upwards or, Seventy Years of An Eventful Life, London, 1910, pp. 6–7.

Two other writers, George Jacob Holyoake and William Hale White, have provided us with descriptions of their native towns. Holyoake was born in Birmingham in 1817, a period when parts of the city were still rural, and had not been swallowed up by factories. In 1892 he described the place of his birth:

'Before our door where I was born stood, on the opposite side, a considerable clump of well-grown trees, amid which was a hatter's working shop. On the adjacent corner of Hurst Street stood the Fox Tavern, as it stands now; but then the sign had been newly painted by a one-armed, short, quick-stepping nervous-faced, dapper artist; and a very wonderful fox it seemed to me. The sharp-nosed, bushy-tailed animal was rushing to cover—on the sign. I had never seen a fox or a cover, except on that sign. I had only seen a workshop, and I envied the fox who had such a paradise to flee to. Yet we were not without glimpses of real nature about us. Below the Fox Tavern was a "Green"; at the bottom was a garden belonging to a house with a gateway, where one of my father's sisters lived. The garden fence was not a dead wall, but a low, wood paling, through which children could see the flowers in the garden. From the end of Inge Street the trees of the parsonage ground made a small wood before us, and apparently in their midst, but really beyond them, arose the spire of the "Old Church"—as we called St. Martin's. On summer afternoons and moonlight nights, the church spire, rising above the nestling trees, presented an aspect of a verdant village church in the midst of the busy workshop town. Down through the "Green", the way led to Lady Well Walk, where more gardens lay, and the well was wide, clear, and deep. Hundreds of times did I fetch water from it. We had a pump in our own yard, but we did not think much of the pump—and we did it no injustice. Gone now— gone long ago—is the glory of the well, and the Lady's Walk, and the "Green", and the Parsonage Ground, and the trees, and church spire. The spire is still about, but the sight of it has been hidden by buildings of every order of deformity. Inge Street, now, looking down from the Horse Fair end, is, as it were, the entrance to a coal-pit, which, when I first knew it, appeared as the entrance to a sylvan glen.'

> *Sixty Years of an Agitator's Life*, Vol. I, London, 3rd ed., 1893.

William Hale White, who was born in Bedford in 1831, wrote as a very old man about the town where he had passed his boyhood. It was the setting for several of his novels and in his autobiography he recalled the town with affection:

'To return to Bedford. In my boyhood it differed, excepting an addition northwards a few years before, much less from Speed's map of 1609 than the Bedford of 1910 differs from the Bedford of 1831. There was but one bridge, but it was not Bunyan's bridge and many of the gabled houses still remained. To our house, much like the others in the High Street, there was no real drainage, and our drinking-water came from a shallow well sunk in the gravelly soil of the back yard. A sewer it is true, ran down the High Street, but it discharged itself at the bridgefoot in the middle of the town, which was full of cesspools. Every now and then the river was drawn off, and the thick masses of poisonous filth which formed its bed were dug out and carted away. In consequence of the imperfect outfall we were liable to tremendous floods. At such times a torrent roared under the bridge, bringing down haystacks, dead bullocks, cows and sheep. Men with long poles were employed to fend the abutments from the heavy blows which struck them. A flood in 1823 was not forgotten for many years. One Saturday night in November a man rode into the town, post-haste from Olney warning all inhabitants of the valley of the Ouse that the "Buckinghamshire Water" was coming down with alarming force, and would soon be upon them. It arrived almost as soon as the messenger, and invaded my uncle Lovell's dining room reaching nearly as high as the top of the table.

'The goods traffic to and from London was carried on by an enormous waggon which made the journey twice a week. Passengers generally travelled by the Times coach, a hobby of Mr Whitbread's. It was horsed with four magnificent cream-coloured horses and did the fifty miles from Bedford to London at very nearly ten miles an hour, or twelve miles actual speed, excluding stoppages for change. Barring accidents it was always punctual to a minute and every evening, except Sundays, exactly as the clock of St Paul's struck eight it crossed the bridge. I have known it wait before entering the town if it was five or six minutes too soon, a kind of polish or artistic completeness being thereby given to a performance in which much pride was taken.'

The Early Life of Mark Rutherford (*W. Hale White*) *by himself*, London, 1913, pp. 13–15.

And so to London. We started with a view of London at the close of the eighteenth century. Here is another description of it at the same period, written from an entirely different standpoint. The author is William Hone, publisher and author, whose autobiography deserves to be better known than it is:

'Paddington was then an inconsiderable village, having a single stage-coach, which daily made one journey to and from the City.

'Our next residence was on the west side of Tottenham Court Road. All beyond Warren Street, which had been lately commenced, was open meadow-land and dairy farms as far as the eye could see, except the "Adam and Eve" then resorted to as a country tea-garden house, at the west corner of the Hampstead Road, and the "Old Kings Head" at the opposite corner, with a few humble buildings.

My young eyes were attracted by the numerous moving objects I beheld from our windows. Opposite was a cow-lair, and great gravel-pits adjoining, while beyond meadows extended to Gray's Inn Lane; one of them conspicuous at a distance, formed the bowling-green, now a public-house, in Cromer Street.

'From far and near on Sunday mornings in the different fields crowds assembled around preachers, boxing-matches, dog-fights, and duck-hunts. To these scenes resorted pickpockets, who, when detected and pursued, were brought by large mobs to ponds in the gravel-pits and mercilessly ducked with uproarious shouting.

'On Sundays London poured towards the country a populous tide of individuals differing much in appearance from our present Sunday swarms to the suburbs; many were personally afflicted, youths walking on crutches, or with one crutch, girls suffering under disorders of the hip-joint, rickety children with jointed iron straps on their legs—at least one tenth of the passers-by were crippled or diseased.

'On Sunday afternoons, tradesmen or respectable journeymen and their wives were profusely powdered. Men wore scarlet coats and long-flapped, figured waistcoats; cocked hats, with their hair behind in long or large clubbed pigtails, and at the side in large stiff curls; silver or plated buckles, curiously wrought or bespangled on their shoes.'

F. W. Hackwood, *William Hone, His Life and Times*, London, 1912, pp. 23–24.

At this point somebody might object that all these extracts were written by men. Were there no memoirs written by women? The simple answer is that there were very few, and certainly none with so keen an awareness of environment. The one book which does tell something about the life of a woman who quarrelled with her father and had to make her own way in the world is *A Narrative of the Life of Mrs. Charlotte Charke*, published in 1755 (a modern reprint is available, 1929). Mrs. Charke was the daughter of Colley Cibber, an actor, and the story of her life is certainly amusing while at the same time telling us a good deal about London life seen, as it were, from below.

One other interesting source of knowledge regarding poor children and how they lived is the series put together by the Central Society of Education in 1836, and published two years later (a modern reprint is available). The Society sought to provide schools, and in order to arouse interest in its projects it published a series of brief biographies of children whom its investigator came across in the streets. One was Elizabeth Knowles, aged fourteen, who lived in Shoreditch:

'Eight in family, Elizabeth the eldest; father works at shoe-making, as chamber master. Went to a charity school Wood Street, Spitalfields; used to have a stuff gown and two pairs of shoes every year given to her; the children only allowed to stay three years in the school; thinks it was a very good school, but used to write only once a week, and sometimes not at all. Cannot now write much. Father is going to send her to evening school to learn to write, as soon as he can afford it. Had Bible from the school which she reads. Her father bought her *Jack the Giant Killer*, *Tom Thumb* and *Robinson Crusoe*. Father and mother cannot read; she used to read to them, of an evening, *Robinson Crusoe*. Was only taught cyphering (arithmetic) once a month; doesn't know how many four times twelve make; was chiefly employed in reading and sewing at school; can hem and stitch and do anything with her needle.'

Central Society of Education Second Publication of
1838, p. 394, Woburn Press reprint, 1968.

Here, then, are some voices from the past. Such people formed the greater part of the population; it was they who walked the streets and lived in the smaller houses so many of which have disappeared.

Let me finally recommend you, if you are interested, to make a point of browsing in the pages of Samuel Pepys' *Diary*, and of any diaries and journals you may come across. *The Life and Times of Anthony à Wood* is a delightful book for dipping into. The irritable Mr. à Wood gives an unforgettable picture of life in seventeenth-century Oxford and many of his pages sparkle with life. It is always worth searching amongst the autobiographies, journals and diaries at your library. If you are lucky you may come across an unpublished one like that of Henry Edward Price, a cabinet maker, which is at Islington. There is much to be enjoyed in this kind of literature.

To sum up, local history is first of all a pleasurable activity in which reading and the discovery of books is combined with looking critically at towns, landscapes and all kinds of features, both natural and man-made. Beyond pleasure, local history—reading and looking—is an activity which will bring us to a deeper understanding of the past we see today.

Appendixes

MUSEUMS

This is a select list of museums and includes only those which in the opinion of the author illustrate 'the past we see today' particularly well. In a sense, of course, most museums do this, but those which are included here offer either a rounded view of life in the past or take a particular aspect and specialize in it. All museums, whether listed here or not, are worth a visit and many, particularly those in provincial centres, will contain exhibits of local-history interest.

In some cases a small charge for admission is made. A number of museums open at irregular hours. Before setting out to visit a specific museum you may find it wise to check both admission charges and times of opening in the books listed on page 108 or in the current issue of the *Libraries, Museums and Art Galleries Year Book*, which you will be able to consult at your library.

ABERDEEN
Provost Skene's House. Exhibits of social and domestic life housed in a seventeenth-century building.

ABINGDON, Berkshire
Borough Museum. Domestic material of the last four centuries, children's toys, costumes and uniforms of the Napoleonic period.

ALTON, Hampshire
The Curtis Museum. Folk-life exhibits, agriculture, crafts, domestic life.

ARMAGH, Northern Ireland
County Museum. Eighteenth- and nineteenth-century costumes, domestic appliances of the past, tools made by blacksmiths.

ASHWELL, near Baldock, Hertfordshire
Ashwell Village Museum. Folk collection: tools of the farmer, blacksmith, shepherd, wheelwright, coachbuilder, carpenter, bricklayer, straw plaiter, pillow lace maker; snuff-boxes, spectacles, pipes.

ASTON MUNSLOW, near Craven Arms, Shropshire
The White House Country Life Museum. Exhibition of domestic articles, furniture, cooking-pots, dairy, etc., in a fourteenth-century timbered hall.

BATH, Somerset
Museum of Costume. The largest and most detailed display of costume in the world. The exhibition is in the Assembly Rooms, a carefully restored eighteenth-century building.

BATLEY, Yorkshire
Oakwell Hall. This is a fine example of an Elizabethan Manor Farm. Period furniture throughout. There are also Civil War connections.

BATTLE, Sussex
Battle and District Historical Society Museum. Battle of Hastings interest, also Sussex iron industry.

BEDFORD
Elstow Moot Hall. Medieval market hall housing seventeenth-century furniture, tapestries. Collection of early editions of books by John Bunyan.

BELFAST, Northern Ireland
Transport Museum. Comprehensive collection of Irish transport.

Ulster Folk Museum. Material relating to town and country in Northern Ireland. A large open-air section contains traditional buildings removed from the countryside and re-erected in natural settings. Agricultural implements, horse-drawn transport, Irish lace, patchwork quilts.

BIBURY, Gloucestershire
Arlington Mill Museum and Art Gallery. Old mill machinery in working order, agricultural implements and country crafts, Victorian and Edwardian furniture, Victorian costumes. N.B. Some cottages in the village are well worth seeing too.

BIDEFORD, Devon
Bideford Public Library and Museum. Ship models, shipwrights' tools.

BIGGAR, Lanarkshire
Gladstone Court. Small indoor street, shops mostly 1820–1880; printer, grocer, shoemaker, druggist, ironmonger, dress-maker, also a small schoolroom.

BIRMINGHAM, Warwickshire
Aston Hall. A Jacobean House, built between 1618 and 1635, in its own park in the city. Period furniture, very fine staircase.

Avery Historical Museum. History of weighing from early Egyptian times to the present.

Blakesley Hall. A timber-framed Yeoman's house built about 1550 to 1600. Contains the Birmingham local-history collection. There are two period rooms, a bedroom and a kitchen.

City Museum and Art Gallery. Exhibition of science and industry from the Industrial Revolution to the present day, machine tools, motor-cars, bicycles, motor cycles, aircraft, early radio and telephone equipment, typewriters, sewing-machines, musical boxes, atomic reactor, etc. A very fine industrial collection with push-button scientific exhibits.

Weoley Castle. Formerly a fortified manor-house built between 1260 and 1280. On the site of an earlier building surrounded by a moat. Museum contains items excavated on the site.

BLACKBURN, Lancashire
Lewis Textile Museum. The textile industry: machinery, accessories, samples, full-scale working models of spinning-jenny, spinning Mule, Arkwright's Water Frame, original hand loom and Lancashire loom, spinning-wheels.

BLANDFORD, Dorset
Royal Signals Museum. History of military communications.

BLEADON, near Weston-super-Mare, Somerset
Yeldingtree Railway Museum Trust. Railways from the beginnings to 1848.

BOLTON, Lancashire
Tonge Moor Textile Machinery Museum. Early cotton machinery; Samuel Crompton's Mule.

BOVINGTON CAMP, near Wareham, Dorset
Royal Armoured Corps Tank Museum. Over 120 tracked and wheeled fighting vehicles from 1809 to 1965, both British and foreign.

BRIGHTON, Sussex
Brighton Motor Museum. Veteran and vintage cars, motor cycles and cycles.

The Royal Pavilion. A Royal palace furnished as it was when George IV was in residence.

Toy Museum. Toys of all periods and all countries.

BRISTOL, Gloucestershire
Georgian House. Built for John Piney, a Bristol sugar merchant, between 1790 and 1792. Eighteenth-century furniture, most of the original fittings. There are a kitchen and a laundry in the basement.

National Postal Museum, E.C.1. Stamps and postal material.

LOOE, Cornwall
Cornish Museum. Cornish life in the past. Arts, crafts, folk-lore, mining, fishing, early travel, lighting, games, pastimes, witchcraft, etc.

MAIDSTONE, Kent
Tyrwhitt-Drake Museum of Carriages. About fifty carriages and their accessories, mechanically driven and horse-drawn.

MANCHESTER
The Gallery of English Costume, Platt Hall. English costume from the seventeenth century to the present. Collection housed in period house of *c.* 1764.

NETHER ALDERLEY, Cheshire
Nether Alderley Mill. Traditional water-mill machinery in operation grinding corn, driven by water power. Traditional items connected with mills and milling.

OLD WARDEN, near Biggleswade, Bedfordshire
Shuttleworth Collection. Aircraft and engines from 1909 to the present. Cars from 1897, bicycles and motor cycles from 1819.

PORTMADOC, Caernarvonshire
Festiniog Railway Museum. Displays and relics illustrating the history of this railway.

READING, Berkshire
University of Reading. Museum of English Rural Life. Agricultural implements, tools and domestic equipment.

RIPON, Yorkshire
Wakeman's House Museum. Local folk museum.

RUFFORD, near Ormskirk, Lancashire
Rufford Old Hall Folk Museum. Medieval hall holding collection of old-time farming implements, domestic appliances, utensils, Victorian dresses, Tudor and Jacobean furniture.

ST. HELENS, Lancashire
Pilkington Glass Museum. The history of glass-making from Egyptian times to the present day.

SALFORD, Lancashire
Science Museum. Science in everyday life. There is a full-scale reproduction of a coal-mine.

STANFORD PARK, near Rugby, Leicestershire
Stanford Hall Motor Cycle and Car Museum. Vintage cars, motor cycles, bicycles, scooters. Also a 1690 house containing antique furniture, costumes and kitchen utensils. Beautiful thirteenth-century church.

STOKE BRUERNE, Northamptonshire
Waterways Museum. Set by a canal, this museum contains relics and souvenirs from the time when inland waterways were an important element in the country's transport system.

SWANSEA, Glamorganshire
Industrial Museum of South Wales. General industrial background of the area. Aluminium, nickel, oil refining, steel and plate manufacture, transport.

SWINDON, Wiltshire
Great Western Railway Museum. History of this company. A special Brunel room contains many items associated with this famous engineer.

THURSFORD, near Fakenham, Norfolk
Organ and Engine Museum. Contains very rare mechanical organs and traction engines; there are organs used by showmen, fixed organs, steam road locomotives used by showmen, general purpose steam traction engines, steam road rollers, ploughing engines.

TOTNES, Devonshire
The Elizabethan House (Totnes Borough Museum). Social and Industrial life in Totnes, also its agricultural development from the thirteenth century onwards. Trade tools, furniture, toys, domestic articles, costumes. Various items connected with the cloth trade.

TOWYN, Merionethshire
The Narrow Gauge Railway Museum. Exhibits concerned with the narrow gauge railways of the British Isles.

WAKEFIELD, Yorkshire
City Museum. Victorian and Jacobean rooms. Costumes. Period shops, and a 'street' comprising a prison cell, a nineteenth-century post office, a Victorian toy-shop and a sixteenth- to nineteenth-century inn.

WARWICK
Doll Museum. Antique and period dolls and toys.

WYE, near Ashford, Kent
Wye College Agricultural Museum. Agricultural implements housed in a tithe barn and oast-house.

YORK
York Castle Museum. Folk Museum of Yorkshire life. Complete reconstructed cobbled streets of shops. Period rooms of craft workshops, working water-driven corn-mill, toys, costumes, crafts, agricultural equipment, etc.

ZENNOR, Cornwall
Wayside Museum. Housed in an old mill, exhibits are concerned with milling, mining, quarrying, fishing, smithying, domestic objects. There is a model tin-mine and an old Cornish open hearth.

Finally, a museum of social and economic life which is in the process of being organized. This is the North of England Open-Air Museum situated at Beamish, six miles south-east of Newcastle upon Tyne, and financed jointly by eight local authorities. A preliminary part of the museum opened on 20 May 1972. Over the next few years the two-hundred acre site will be developed in a series of 'areas'—such as urban, rural, coal, lead and iron. Within each area, appropriate old buildings from all parts of the North will be rebuilt and equipped with the kind of machinery or furniture they once held. It is hoped that the exhibits, which range from a miner's kettle on the hob to a complete colliery, will eventually provide a panorama of life over two centuries in this part of England. The Museum Director, to whom I am indebted for this information, is Mr. Frank Atkinson.

ORDNANCE SURVEY MAPS

The Ordnance Survey Map Catalogue is available free on request from the Director General, Ordnance Survey, Leatherhead Road, Chessington, Surrey; or from Edward Stanford Limited, 12–14 Long Acre, London, W.C.2.

A very wide range of maps is published, and you will find the historical ones of especial interest. These include:

Southern Britain in the Iron Age	*Ancient Britain—South*
Roman Britain	*Britain in the Dark Ages*
Map of Hadrian's Wall	*Monastic Britain—North*
Ancient Britain—North	*Monastic Britain—South*

Ordnance Survey publications can be ordered from most booksellers, some of whom, if they are Ordnance Survey Agents, may carry a stock.

SOME BOOKS TO BE CONSULTED

In addition to the books mentioned in some of the chapters, and the notes on forming your own reference collection, here is a short list of books which you will certainly find useful.

James Arnold, *The Shell Book of Country Crafts*, John Baker, 1968. A book to dip into. It is well illustrated and contains a great deal of information about country life and its crafts.

Courtney Dainton, *Clock Jacks and Bee Boles*, Phoenix, 1957. 'A dictionary of country sights'—out of print, but well worth looking for in second-hand bookshops.

Eilert Ekwall, *The Concise Oxford Dictionary of English Place-Names*, Oxford at the Clarendon Press, 1960. This is a marvellous book to which I have already referred. You will find the same author's smaller work, *Street-Names of the City of London*, Oxford at the Clarendon Press, 1954, equally fascinating and helpful.

G. E. Evans, *The Farm and the Village*, Faber, 1969. An admirable study of rural life, illustrated with plates and drawings.

Arnold Fellows, *The Wayfarer's Companion*, Oxford, 1937 (and reprints).

Geoffrey Fletcher, *The London Nobody Knows*, Hutchinson, 1962; Penguin, 1965.

John Haddon, *Discovering Towns*, Shire Publications, 1970. A 92-page pamphlet to which I have already referred. Quite the best introduction to learning about towns that I have come across.

W. G. Hoskins, *Local History in England*, Longmans, 1959. This is the standard work on the subject. Written with knowledge and enthusiasm by a great historian. If you are seriously interested in local history you will have to read this book sooner or later. At all events you should dip into it.

W. G. Hoskins, *The Making of the English Landscape*, Hodder and Stoughton, 1955. (A paperback edition is published by Penguin Books.) The 83 plates and 17 maps in it make this book one that you should at least look into. Like the other book by Professor Hoskins, mentioned above, this one is written with knowledge and enthusiasm. It is also one that will give you great enjoyment.

Kenneth Hudson, *Industrial Archaeology*, University Paperbacks, Methuen, 1965. A very informative introduction to studying the relics of the Industrial Revolution. This is a comparatively new subject and is of obvious interest to local historians. There is a useful book list and some instructions on recording what you see.

John Penoyre & Michael Ryan, *The Observer's Book of Architecture*, Warne Revised Ed., 1958.

Michael Storm, *Urban Development*, Oxford 1965. An introduction to towns, illustrated with maps, plans and photographs.

Eric S. Wood, *Collins Field Guide to Archaeology*, Collins, 1963. An extremely useful handbook which takes a very wide view of the term 'archaeology'. A book for reference and for pleasure.

The County History series published by Darwen Finlayson Ltd. is very useful. It is well worth inquiring whether the county you live in is included.

THINGS TO DO

Archaeological Excavations
If you are over sixteen and keen on history, you may be able to join a team digging in search of the past. In order to find out when and where there is digging, you should contact the Council for British Archaeology, who publish a calendar of excavations at the beginning of each month. Their address is 8 St. Andrew's Place, London, N.W.1. The subscription to the calendar is reasonable.

It is also worth remembering that if you are too young to dig, at many of the larger excavations visitors are shown round and told what is happening.

Seeing Country Crafts
If you are keen on seeing craftsmen at work, the Council for Small Industries in Rural Areas publishes an excellent list indicating where they are to be found. It is called *The Visitor's Guide to Country Workshops in Britain*, and can be had, free, if you send a foolscap stamped, addressed envelope to the Council at 35 Camp Road, Wimbledon, London, S.W. 19.

Index